George Gilman Smith

The boy in gray

A story of the war

George Gilman Smith

The boy in gray
A story of the war

ISBN/EAN: 9783337282684

Printed in Europe, USA, Canada, Australia, Japan

Cover: Foto ©ninafisch / pixelio.de

More available books at **www.hansebooks.com**

A STORY OF THE WAR.

BY

GEO. G. SMITH,
Chaplain of Phillips's Legion, Georgia Volunteers,
Author of " Harry Thornton," " Berry's Triumph," " Mr. Hall and His Family," etc.

MACON, GA.:
MACON PUBLISHING COMPANY.
1894.

DEDICATION.

To the Sons of the Veterans,

WHETHER THEY WORE THE GRAY OR WORE THE BLUE,

THIS BOOK

IS AFFECTIONATELY DEDICATED BY

THE AUTHOR.

PREFACE.

THIS book has been written for the young people who are interested in the story of the stirring scenes through which their fathers passed.

It is needless to say that it is not a true record of personal life; it is no more history than is "Robinson Crusoe" or the "Pilgrim's Progress." The facts stated as historic are to be relied upon. Many of these came under my own eye, when I went over the ground which Roger speaks of in his campaign. The pictures of "Georgia life" are, I think, correctly drawn, and ought not to fade out entirely.

This little book has been written in the interest of peace, and I have been anxious that the Southern boys and girls who will be largely and almost exclusively my readers should see not only how nobly their fathers bore themselves in the war, and how grandly their mothers and sisters toiled at home, but that they should see how really noble and generous were many of those who were on the other side. If any one should object that these characters had no counterparts in real life, I can only say that they have not heard the whole story and that, while such cases were too rare, there were such. The absence of malice between the soldiers was a remarkable feature of the contest; and if there has been feelings of bitterness between the North and the South, it is high time for them to have an end. The children of the old English people who settled America, whether they landed at Jamestown or Plymouth Rock, have too much in common to be at enmity now. Common dangers are too near them for them to vex each other.

One terrific war is enough. Let us have peace and brotherhood for evermore; but a peace purchased by falsehood or by suppression of the truth is no peace, and a true story is the only one that should be told. I have tried to tell it, and I should feel sad if I thought I had said anything to divide the young people, North and South, whom I would so gladly see united.

Geo. G. Smith.

Macon (Vineville), Ga.

CONTENTS.

	Page
CHAPTER I. The Lawsons...................................	11
CHAPTER II. A Gathering of the Clouds.....................	19
CHAPTER III. "Ivy Bush".....................................	35
CHAPTER IV. A Chapter Which I Wish Could Be Left Out............	50
CHAPTER V. Some Pleasing Events.........................	62
CHAPTER VI. A Rather Dull but an Important Chapter.................	67
CHAPTER VII. The War Drum................................	74
CHAPTER VIII. Helen..	86
CHAPTER IX. Gaining Experience...........................	93
CHAPTER X. A Week at Home..............................	104
CHAPTER XI. Campaigning on the Coast.....................	110
CHAPTER XII. Infantry Service in Northern Virginia...................	117
CHAPTER XIII. Things in Liberty.............................	131
CHAPTER XIV. Maryland! My Maryland.......................	134
CHAPTER XV. "Yank" and "Johnny" in the Same Hospital............	139
CHAPTER XVI. The Army Again—Winter Quarters...................	146

Chapter XVII.
The American Waterloo.................................. 151

Chapter XVIII.
Hospital Life 154

Chapter XIX.
"Pine Lodge" Again................................ 161

Chapter XX.
Prison Life................................... 164

Chapter XXI.
Wave upon Wave............................... 170

Chapter XXII.
Free at Last................................ 180

Chapter XXIII.
Midnight.................................. 185

Chapter XXIV.
Beginning Anew.............................. 188

Chapter XXV.
Some Unlooked-for Events.............................. 200

Chapter XXVI.
How Bob Durham Lost His Case 204

Chapter XXVII.
At the Bottom of the Ladder............................ 210

Chapter XXVIII.
Roger Lawson, Attorney at Law....................... 216

Chapter XXIX.
A Dark Chapter in American History................... 231

Chapter XXX.
Get Thee Behind Me, Satan 238

Chapter XXXI.
Some Surprises................................ 243

Chapter XXXII.
May Flowers........ 250

Chapter XXXIII.
Orange Flowers.. 263

CHAPTER I.

THE LAWSONS.

ROGER LAWSON, the first of the name who settled in Georgia, came with the Puritan colony from Dorchester, in South Carolina, about 1755; and settled an estate of one thousand acres on Midway River in what was then St. John's Parish. He brought with him thirty black slaves, who began at once to clear the land; and as the range was good, the large stock of cattle he drove into it fared well from the first, and they rapidly increased, and his rice fields were soon put in good condition; and when he died the second Roger found a large rice plantation, well equipped, and a hundred slaves as his heritage, and now, after over a hundred years, the third Roger was at the old home. Long ago the first home, a log cabin, had been torn away; and now a comfortable and comely mansion, built by the second Roger, father of the present owner, stood among the live oaks on the bluff. It was an old colonial mansion, with broad verandas and roomy halls and immense wide-mouthed chimneys. The mantels, which were brought from England, were carved with the quaint carving of a century ago, and the mansion doors were of English oak. The brick in the chimneys, the glass in the windows, the doors and mantels, came from beyond the sea, but all else had come from the plantation; and though the house had stood for a hundred years, yet, save a repainting and overhauling now and then, and a recovering every thirty years, it was as the second builder left it.

A group of neat buildings, high from the ground and comfortably furnished, were the abiding places of the household servants, of whom there seems to us of this day a rather excessive number; for there was Robert, the master's butler; and Mary, the maid of the mistress; and Nancy, the house girl; and Jack, dining room boy; and the chief cook, Judy; and her assistant, Chloe; and Dick, the stable boy; and old Mammy and the two seamtresses; and over all was Uncle Jack, who was Mammy's husband, and had been, he said, "old Massa's man servant in de late war," when he was in "de camp wid him." The late war was 1812, and it was now 1860, but it was the late war yet to Uncle Jack.

Roger Lawson the third, better known as Capt. Lawson, was a wealthy rice planter, as his father had been before him. He was now near fifty years old, and had graduated from the State University thirty years before, where Alex H. Stephens was his classmate. Born in affluence and with all the advantages which social position could give him, he was yet brought up to habits of industry and early taught self-reliance.

Old Roger was a somewhat stern man of the old Puritan type, and he and his wife were devout members of Dr. McWhir's church at Midway, and they had trained the boy most carefully. There were no Sunday schools then; but Sunday was regarded as a holy day at "Lawson Place," and kept with Puritan exactness. The Shorter Catechism had been carefully studied by the children and faithfully committed to memory, and Roger and his sisters were thoroughly acquainted with the somewhat, to them, inscrutable teachings of the Westminster Assembly.

Roger was a fine young fellow when he left the high school for Athens, and here he fell in with a good set. Charles Jones, his neighbor, and Tom Ginlat, from the adjoining county, and Alex Stephens, the wonder of the college, influenced him for good, and when the great revival came on in Athens he was converted, and Dr. Hoyt received him into the Presbyterian Church.

Mary Maxwell, who lived on the adjoining estate, was an only daughter and inherited the broad acres of her father, Col. Maxwell, and was not only an heiress, but a lovely Christian girl, who had come from Dr. Marks's school at Barhamville, S. C., finely accomplished the summer before Roger graduated. It was inevitable that Roger Lawson and Mary Maxwell should wed, and wed they did, much to the joy of the parents of Roger and of the widowed mother of Mary. That was in 1838, just after Roger left college. The good people of "Lawson Place" did not live long after the happy event, and for this score of years Capt. Roger had been in charge of the two plantations. There were two large quarters in charge of a manager. In each there were about twenty neat little whitewashed cottages with a garden of an acre or more attached. In these cabins, as they were called, the negroes lived, and at the head of the avenue was the comfortable six-room house of the manager. The rice fields stretched along the river for a mile, and the large canals and small ditches divided them into beautiful plats which were planted in rice. There were one hundred negroes on each place, but of these there were a number of children and old people who did but little work.

Capt. Lawson was a very kind master. He saw to it that his slaves were well fed and well clad, and their religion and their morals were carefully looked after. He had a neat chapel on his land built entirely by himself. The Baptist preacher and the Methodist missionary each had an appointment there, and were paid by him, and his wife and himself and his daughter taught the little ones in Sunday school.

I should fail to do my duty as a fair chronicler if I did not tell as true what the world has persisted in believing for a long time could not but be false: that these slaves of Capt. Lawson, and of such as he, were better fed, better clad, better trained, and were more moral and more religious and more cultured, than the same number of farm laborers in any other part of the world, but so it was. They were not permitted to do as they wished, and alas! I have found that when people, young or old, black or white, are permitted to do as they wish, many of them wish to go wrong. They were made to work, and alas! it is a sad fact that many people will not work unless they are made to do so. The Captain's people said they loved him, and he said that he loved them, and I am sure that he did.

However much he might lose in his planting

ventures or however much he might be embarrassed, his people had never known any difference in his treatment of them. Their rations and their clothing and their medical attendance were always sure. The Captain was not a money-making man. He lived in comfort, and gave generously, and sometimes disasters unlooked for came and pressed him sorely, and this was one of those times. For two successive years the floods from the river had covered his rice, and the whole crop had been lost. He had made large outlay for a rice mill and a steam engine, and the crops failing, he had been compelled to go largely in debt. This he had no difficulty in doing, but a $20,000 debt is not a pleasant thing to carry, and he felt its burden.

The two older children of Capt. Lawson died in infancy, and Helen, the daughter, and young Roger, the son, were the only children now in the family. Helen was a lovely, brown-eyed girl of eighteen, and Roger a bright, handsome, merry boy of sixteen. Helen had just returned from the school of Dr. Marks at Barhamville, where her mother, twenty years before her birth, had been educated. Roger had attended the old Medway academy, and was now ready for the university. In the summer time Capt. Lawson went with his family to the mountains of Georgia, and settled them for four months on the banks of the Sequee, in Habersham County. Here, three miles from Clarksville, he had a cosy home, on which he kept a few negroes and a few horses and some cattle. It was a retreat from the miasma of the swamp, and a pleasant change from lowland to upland.

Capt. Lawson had his title from being captain of the Liberty Troop. This was a small company of volunteer cavalry, which was composed of the gentlemen of the county. It had been in continuous existence since the first American Revolution, and was the pride of the Liberty people.

The Captain was an old time gentleman. He had mingled only with that class in his youth: and from his father, who was his constant companion, he had imbibed the views and habits of an old time English country gentleman. Save that he was a Presbyterian of the nineteenth century, he was really a reproduction of Sir Roger de Coverly. He was a Whig in politics, and thoroughly conservative. He kept up too the manners of the century before. The old sideboard of his father was still in its place, and the cut glass decanter of cognac brandy sat upon it now in 1860 as it had been in 1790. The visitor had opened for him a bottle of old wine and had prepared for him a brandy toddy, as it had been done for his father's guest.

In his family life he took with no new ways. The card table was wheeled out in the evening, and father and mother and son and daughter joined in a game of old-fashioned whist. They went to church every Sunday, and were careful in their Sabbath observance. He was thoroughly an upright man, and she was thoroughly a good woman. He had great respect for old traditions, and little use for new things. He never drank to excess, and his good wife had seen him take his thimbleful of brandy and his glass of wine for all these years. I do not mention these facts to commend them, on the contrary I disapprove of them, but I mention them that I may show how good people lived over forty years ago.

CHAPTER II.

A GATHERING OF THE CLOUDS.

IT was now June. The time for the family to leave Liberty for Habersham was generally the the 15th, and Capt. Lawson was making his arrangements to go. To provide for over two hundred people for several months required management and money. The failure of his rice crop for two years successively had rendered it necessary for Capt. Lawson to buy largely of Western corn and bacon, and the large outlay for these things was giving him very considerable anxiety. The firm of Robert Harris & Co., of Savannah, had been the factors of his father and of his grandfather, and he had with them unbounded credit, but it had become evident that he must negotiate a considerable loan or be seriously straitened, and they had been employed to do it for him, and this day in June he had received their reply. He handed it to his wife.

SAVANNAH, GA., May 31, 1860.

CAPT. ROGER LAWSON.

Dear Captain: We herewith send you account of sales of ten bales of Sea Island cotton and of the lot of rice sent by sloop " Margaret." We have communicated with our New

York correspondents, Messrs. Fall, Daniel & Co., and they say that they have arranged for the $20,000 you desire to borrow, but say that the mortgage of the *plantation and negroes* will not be satisfactory. The old Quaker who proposes to let you have the money for five years at six per cent. is not willing to take security of this kind; but if you will give him a mortgage on the two plantations, and not include the negroes, this will be satisfactory. We are sure that unless there should be a a strange succession of bad years you will be able to pay the amount easily in the five years, and as we know how reluctant you are to mortgage your family slaves, we have written to our New York friends that they could assure their correspondent that you would accept his terms.

Very truly yours,   ROBERT HARRIS & Co.

Mrs. Lawson read the letter. The shade of anxiety and of concern which crossed her face soon passed away, and she calmly said: "Well, dear, you can do no better than this; it is one of those things which must be done."

"Yes, my love, it must be done; but I do not like to do it. The certainty of paying the note is as good as it can be, for I can sell a part of the lower place, with the hands on it, to Sam Varnadoe for $20,000 to-morrow, and not have to borrow any money, but I cannot part with my old slaves. I am afraid that they would not be content; for while Sam is as good a master as I am, he was not brought up with the negroes, as I was, and I cannot bear the thought of selling them to anybody.

But have you thought of one thing? that lower place does not belong to me."

"It doesn't? Well, to whom does it belong?"

"I made a marriage settlement, and secured it to you."

"Well, can't I mortgage it then?"

"No, for it doesn't belong to you."

"Well, who does own it?"

"Both of us."

"Well then, we both will mortgage it. I am not going to have you so bothered any longer. Every time you have had a letter from Mr. Harris you've seemed to be as blue as indigo."

"Well, I could not help it. These various little debts which I could not pay, and the $10,000 I had borrowed from the bank through the Harrises, have harassed me more than I can tell; but this loan will relieve me, and by careful living we can doubtless pay it all before the day it is due. We will, however, have to go to Hinesville to make the papers."

When the trip was made they called at the office of Judge Law, who drew the mortgage. After it was signed Captain Lawson said: "Judge, I want you now to make a deed of gift for me. I do not know what may happen, and I do not know that she will ever need it, but I want to make a settlement on my wife. The plantation just mortgaged was hers; and if I were to die, and that mortgage were not paid, she might be homeless. I want you to make a deed of gift of my place in Habersham, five hundred acres of land, with all my family plate, furniture, books, stock, cattle, horses, and hogs, to Mary Maxwell Lawson."

"No, Judge, don't do it," said his wife. "I have nothing separate from Roger. I do not want that summer home."

"Don't listen to her, Judge. Make that deed, I say, and make it now, and I will put it on record when I go to Clarksville. I will not feel easy till it is done."

"Well, Captain, it is rather a strange freak that a man worth two hundred thousand dollars should be so anxious about settling a home not worth three thousand dollars on his wife, but I will do as you wish."

And so the deed was drawn. The mortgage was sent on, the money received and placed with the Harrises, and the debts paid; and with lighter hearts the family began to make preparation for the journey to Habersham.

With the mail which brought the letters from Messrs. Harris & Co. came the *Savannah Republican*, and it gave a vivid account of the Charleston

Convention of the Democratic party, and of the split in that great organization. "This," said the Captain sadly, as he laid down the paper, "is the beginning of the end. The Democratic party is hopelessly divided. The Republican will be victorious and abolitionism will be on top and the Union will fall."

"Why, my dear," said his wife, "what is the reason you talk so? You were never a Democrat, and the mere choice of a Republican, bad as that would be, would surely not result as you think."

"Well, maybe not; we shall see what we see. Well, let us leave politics alone and get ready for our trip. What do you say to our going through the country in our carriage?"

"Nothing would please me better. How long will it take us?"

"We can make the journey easily in a week or ten days. And it will give our children a better idea of Georgia. We may have some rather rough fare a part of the way, but the pleasure of going through the country will more than compensate for that."

The children were delighted at the prospect, and the arrangements were made for the start. The plain, strong, comfortable carriage used to convey the family to church, which was drawn by a pair of Kentucky horses, was brought into use for Mrs. Lawson, Helen, and Mammy. The wagon with its two mules carried the baggage and the other servants, and Capt. Lawson and Roger had each his saddle horse. The travelers had a journey of two hundred miles before them, but they were well equipped for pleasant traveling, and could take their own time. They left "Lawson Place" in the early morning, and were soon in the pine woods moving slowly on their way.

There are few parts of Georgia where there is less variety in scenery than in the pine woods of the lower part of the State. There is a gently undulating plain covered with forests of pines and with a carpet of grass now and then crossed by creeks, along whose borders grow the oaks, moss clad, and whose translucent waters have a strange inky tint, and small brooks which gently move over the white sand, and along whose banks are magnolias and bays. The sward of the forest is bedecked with flowers of great beauty. There were few evidences of animal life, save the birds and a few small cattle which were grazing in the ranges. There were but few homes, and they were very small and plain. Rapid traveling was impossible on account of the heavy sand, and night time found them still in Liberty; but they found good quarters in the home of a friend of the Captain, who was a member of the same troop. He was a plain pine woods farmer, but he and his good wife soon made the travelers at home. The supper was generous and well served, and the men lit their pipes and sat on the front piazza and talked of politics and of county matters; and the farmer's wife and the planter's wife chatted of those things which interest women. Few homes were more comfortable than those of independent farmers like John Jones, and few people were more content or more useful than such people. These families had few comforts which the farm did not furnish, but they did not miss them. They cured their own bacon, made their own sugar and sirup, had their own cows, and made their own butter. They had fowls in large numbers, and caught fish at will from the neighboring ponds, and the fields and woods furnished them with small game. The wife had never been far from home, nor did she care to go. She knew how to weave, to spin, to raise fowls, to direct the cook in preparing a savory meal, or if need be to prepare one herself. She made her husband's clothing and that of her children. And while five thousand dollars might have bought all John Jones had, he had enough to make him thoroughly independent; and while he knew that the Captain he entertained could have bought all he owned with half a year's income, that he was college bred while he could barely read, yet he felt no embarrassment and had no sense of inferiority to his guest in entertaining him, and he would have felt as little being entertained by him; and so it was with Nancy Jones, his wife. She had met Mrs. Lawson at Taylor's Creek camp meeting, and entertained her there, and now she gladly welcomed her into her roomy and comfortable log house and entertained with as much simple heartiness as if she did not know any difference in social conditions; and her strong-armed boys just from the field and her rosy-cheeked girls greeted Helen and Roger with hearty cheer, and while the Captain and the Sergeant were on the porch and the matrons were in the family room the young folks were having as merry a game of thimble and blind man's buff as if they had known each other all the years gone by.

"Well, Captain," said Serg. Jones, emptying his pipe, "it's about bedtime, and if you will come into wife's room we'll have a word of prayer."

They came in, and the Bible was taken down from the shelf. "Captain," he said politely, "will you take the book?"

"No; excuse me, Sergeant. I am a pretty good Presbyterian, but I am afraid I am rather a poor Christian, and can't pray in public; but we will be glad to join with you in worship."

The Sergeant took the book. He read his chapter, not always pronouncing the words correctly, but he did his best, and then gave out the hymn, "A Charge to Keep I Have," and the family sung with a hearty devotion, if not with classic elegance, and retired to rest.

I have tried to give this account of the intercourse of the wealthy and cultivated of the Georgia people with their plainer neighbors, that I may show how hearty was the sympathy between them in these olden times. John Jones's brother William had been an overseer for the Captain for years, and while Mrs. Jones and Mrs. Lawson met as equals and there was no envy between them, yet they were not silly enough not to see that their social position was very different, and the paths of the two rarely crossed. The next day early the travelers were on their way through Tattnall, to find very different quarters for the next night's resting.

It was a weary day. Through beds of sand and long slushes they moved, and at nightfall found themselves in the sand hills of Tattnall. Squire

McGinnis had the only house where a traveler could find shelter in that section, and when they reached the Squire's they found a log house with one room for the dwelling, and a kitchen of the same size near by. This was the only chance for entertainment. The Squire was kind enough, and said that they might stay, and his five grown daughters and his good wife were as kind as they knew how to be; but to the mother and Helen the landscape bore a somewhat gloomy outlook. Supper was coming on, and the keen eye of Mrs. Lawson saw that the prospect for a scant meal was very promising, and with a woman's tact she said to the mistress of the cabin: "Let my servant help you to get supper; and if you have some fresh eggs, we have some light bread and coffee and cold ham, and we can make out nicely."

The supper provided by the Squire's wife was fat bacon, collard greens, and corn bread and corn coffee; and the added store from the large lunch basket excited some gratitude, as well as wonder.

"Well, ma'am, I am obleeged to ye. We poor folks can't do as well as we'd like to, and then I don't know as whether we allers does as well as we mout; but sich as we have you is mighty welcome to."

"Thank you, ma'am," said the guest. "We

have done very well; but as I am quite tired, I would like to go to bed as soon as convenient."

"Yes, sartainly. Youns go in thar, and my ole man and me and the gals will come in here. The boys (you hain't seen 'em yit) they is been out arter a bunch of cattle, and when they come in they will sleep outen the shed."

"Well, Captain," said the Squire, "while the women is gittin' ready to go to bed, we'll sit out here, and while you smoke I'll chaw. Whar is you from?"

"From Liberty."

"O yes, I have been down in Libuty. I was a delegit to the Beard's Creek Association last year. You warn't thar, was ye?"

"No, Squire; I did not go."

"Well, I did not think ye was. An old side Baptist I is, and my daddy was afore me. What is you?"

"A Presbyterian."

"A Prisbyteran? Well, I have hearn of them: but I hain't never seen none before, and I 'spose you is a Whig?"

"Well, yes."

"Well, I'm a Dimocrat, a regular Andrew Jackson Dimocrat. I tell you, Captain, when a man is a jestice of the peace, a Baptist deacon, and a rale old ironside Dimocrat, I think that will do. But I 'spect you is purty tired, and so I'll go in the kitchen, and let you and Bud thar go in to bed." And the Squire left his guest.

The Squire settled his home when the pine forests on the sand hills of lower Georgia were counted as valueless except for their pasturage; but he had a hundred head of cattle now, and enriched a few acres of land every year, on which he raised some corn and sugar cane and potatoes. He knew nothing of comfort, and cared nothing for it. Twenty dollars a year paid all his store bills; and all else they needed was made at home. The homespun frocks of the girls, they wove themselves, and the one suit of jeans which the boys wore in winter, and the heavy cotton they wore in summer, were made at home by the old lady. They drove some cattle to the Savannah market every year, and carried some wool; and brought back a few bundles of "spun truck" (as they called yarn), some indigo and madder to dye with, a few tools, some powder and shot, a calico dress for the old woman and each of the girls, a little coffee, and alas! a keg of whisky; and the remainder of the proceeds from his produce he turned into gold, which he carried back to Tattnall and loaned out. He had no expense for newspapers or magazines or schools or churches, and so Squire McGinnis was, despite his poor land, a substantial man, who had money at interest, and whose word in matters of business was as good as his bond.

The fare he furnished the travelers was not the best; but the price of the entertainment was in proportion to its excellence, for when the Captain called for his bill in the morning the whole sum asked was one dollar for everything.

"Say, Captain," said the Squire in a low voice, "won't you come out here a minute?" When he did he said: "I've got a jug of good corn juice, and I thought maybe you'd like a dram. I have to be kind of secret about it sence my Jim is got so fond of the stuff that I have to hide my jug from him. I tell you, Captain, whisky is mighty good if you can take it like I do, but young folks is not to be trusted these days."

"Thank you, Squire; please excuse me." A shadow passed over the Captain's face, and he thought: "Suppose Roger should do like Jim. What?"

The supper and breakfast had been more easily arranged for than a comfortable sleeping place. Geese feathers may be good material to make beds for the winter months; but in June, and in the narrow confines of a log cabin, they are not best suited to promote sound slumber, and when the Captain and Roger saw the prospect of sleeping on small feather beds in a close room they retired and left the house to the mother and Helen and the maid, and with their saddle blankets and some small pillows made themselves comfortable on the front piazza, if such the shelter before the door might be called. The good ladies did not attempt to sleep on the beds of down, but made what we people of the South call "pallets" on the floor; but the Squire's family never knew that their generous self-sacrifice in giving up the feather beds to company had been ignored.

In a good humor the journey began the next day. There were two more long drives before the more thickly settled parts of middle Georgia were reached, but there were good stopping places and kindly entertainment along the route. In those days every planter's home was open to travelers. There were no inns save in the towns, and the man who owned a hundred slaves and kept his carriage opened his door readily to the traveler. If he could pay with true politeness, he charged him for his entertainment. From the pine woods and the wire grass the travelers came into the older counties, with their large plantations and handsome homes. The first settlers of Georgia were poor people, and the beautiful domain was divided into small farms. These were distributed by lot, and many of them were occupied by those who drew them; but the early settlers were a restless race, and the farms were sold and bought by those content to stay until the plantation took the place of the farm, and where many men had owned farms of two hundred acres each one man became the owner of a plantation of one thousand and sometimes of five thousand acres. The veracious chronicler of the Lawsons has sometimes in his early days gone for miles along a highway every foot of which was owned by one planter. These large tracts were divided into different settlements, upon each of which a body of slaves were placed under the charge of an overseer, who was always a white man. The planter's home was generally handsome and comfortable. It was often a large, square wooden building painted white, with broad verandas front and rear. The halls were wide and the rooms large. A great open fireplace blazed with hickory logs in the winter; and in summer windows and doors were, without fear of thieves, thrown open wide. The old plantation houses in Georgia are, alas! disappearing, and where there was once almost every mile a delightful home there is now merely a range of somewhat squalid houses peopled by the negro tenants of the capitalist who has become the possessor of a score of holdings. Our travelers found sufficient comfort on the way; but there was little to interest, and at last, after ten days of easy journeying, the family were at their summer home.

CHAPTER III.

"IVY BUSH."

"IVY BUSH" was the name of Capt. Lawson's summer place. It was a neat little cottage nestling at the base of ivy-clad hills. A fertile valley stretched away to the river, which here came bounding over the rocks, forming a shoal of great beauty. The hills lying back from the cottage were not fertile, but they were covered with a beautiful forest in which, at this season of the year, the woodland flowers were in rich profusion: the laurel, the ivy, the red woodbine, the trumpet flower, and the wild honeysuckles, which were still in bloom in high places, though it was early in the summer.

Here among the cedars and mountain pines and oaks was "Ivy Bush" cottage. It was plain but comfortable, and was well though plainly furnished. A favorite servant who lived with his family on the place winter and summer kept things ready for the coming owner. There were hay and clover in the barn, home-cured meats in the smokehouse, and a garden full of early vegetables waiting for the family. It was indeed a cosy nook in which to hide away, and the tired travelers enjoyed it fully. Captain Lawson had bought the place five years before, and had improved it by removing the unsightly log hut in which the former owner had lived and by building the present cottage. He kept it merely for a retreat from low-country heats, and spent from June to November at it. There were a hundred acres of good valley land; the rest was in forest. The village of Clarksville was three miles away, but on the hills around him some families from middle and lower Georgia had settled summer residences. It was, perhaps, to be regretted that these people were numerous enough to make up a circle of their own, and that they did not intermix with the people native to the county to a greater extent; for generally people who know least of each other think least of each other, especially if they are neighbors, and many a quarrel might have been prevented if the people who engaged in it had been thrown under the same roof for a week before it began. The low-country people called the up-country people "Crackers," and the up-country people retaliated by calling them "Stuck-up High Flyers." The families had but little intercourse with each other; but it so happened that Squire Bass, a substantial old farmer whose place adjoined Capt. Lawson's had been closely connected with the Captain in some business affairs, and the Captain had been entertained at his home, and so the two families had become on quite good terms. The old Squire was one of the best specimens of an up-country farmer. Religious, sensible, decided, kind-hearted, pushing, industrious, and withal well to do, he lived in great comfort in his double log house, around which were four hundred acres of arable land. His grass and grain grew in the valley, and his hillsides were for pasturage. Forty years before he had moved from Rutherford County, N. C., to the woods of Habersham and settled on the very tract of land on which he lived now. He brought with him his rosy-cheeked bride. Peggy Burns was her name before she married. She was only sixteen and he was eighteen when they were wed, and for near fifty years they two had journeyed hand in hand together. When they came to the wilds she was a bride, and she bravely stood by him in all his early struggles. It was a hard life at first. The trees were to be felled, the cabin to be built, and the crop to be made; and she had brought him no dowry, and he had only means enough to buy his land. Her old mother gave her a spinning wheel and a loom, and she knew how to use them; and for all these years the Squire had never worn any clothing her loom did not weave and her needle did not make. His rich son from Atlanta sent him a suit of broadcloth, tailor made, but he left it in the great hair-covered trunk and wore his brown jeans suit still, Aunt Peggy, as everybody called her, was a stout old body of sixty-five. Her house was as neat as a pin. The floors were covered with rag carpet woven by her own hand, and the beds were covered with woolen counterpanes of blue checks in winter, with homemade spreads of snowy whiteness in summer. Everything told of her love of neatness and order. They had no well: but a spring bubbling at the foot of a white oak sent a merry brook toward the river, and a huge trough of poplar into which the refreshing current ran furnished a receptacle for her crocks of milk and butter. The hillside had on it a magnificent orchard of apples and cherries, and a row of huge walnut trees which the good man of the house had planted thirty years before was in the lane in front of the house. They were contented and happy old people who had brought up a large family. All their children were gone from them now but the baby boy, Jimmy I shall call him. He was twenty years old, but he was their baby boy still. There were half a dozen negro slaves on the place. When the Squire came to Habersham he had none; but his wife's mother died, and a black man and his wife were their legacy. They had never bought a slave and never sold one; but as the children went from them they each took with them one of the negroes who had been brought up with them, and now old Joe and Kitty and the four boys were left at the home. I have lingered long around this old homestead; in truth, I am loath to leave it. How many happy hours have I spent under this hospitable roof! No wonder Capt. Lawson loved the old people, and no wonder his wife was a favorite with Mrs. Lawson and Helen. The Squire was a stanch Methodist and a class leader, and Aunt Peggy had been one before him, and all their children followed them. The Lawson children had learned to love these good old people, and Roger was an especial favorite with the old Squire, and indeed Roger was a boy to be fond of. He was so bright, so generous, so brave, so unsuspicious, just such a boy as makes one who knows boys anxious lest he be ruined by a wicked world. The first visitor to the Lawsons after they reached Habersham was the Squire. Jimmy attended to the farm now, and his father took the world easy. He had an old horse, Ball was his name, which he had raised from a colt and which his own hand had fed for these fourteen years; and when Ball was seen hitched you might be sure the Squire was near by. The Lawsons had not fairly finished breakfast the day after they came when Roger called out: "There is old Ball at the gate and there is the Squire!" And he ran to give a hearty greeting to his old friend. "Come in, Squire. We are so glad to see you. How is Aunt Peggy? and how is Jimmy? and how is Trip? and"—

"Bless you, boy, give me a chance to blow. They is all well, and how's your folks? Glad you is all back to Habersham."

"Well, come in. We are just at breakfast. Won't you come and have some?"

"Have breakfast? you lazy folks; why Jeems is been in the bottom a plowin' this two hour. I've had breakfast three hour ago. But where's your pappy?"

"Here he comes now; he'll be awful glad to see you, and there is mamma and Helen."

The old gentleman received a hearty greeting from them all.

"Well, Squire, I am much obliged to you for seeing after things, and as you won't let me pay you, Helen and Mary have brought you and Aunt Peggy a little present, and I made Jack put in the wagon a little sack of rice as a present for you."

"Yes, Uncle Bass," said Helen, "I have brought you a pair of spectacles. I told the jeweler to give me some strong Presbyterian ones, so you could read the Bible right; and here is Aunt Peggy's present," giving him a New Testament of extra large print beautifully bound in Turkey morocco."

"You brought me some Prisbyteran glasses, did you, you sassy gal? Well, they'll have to be mighty strong before I can see any of your Prisbyteran doctrine about election in the Testament. Well, won't Peggy be proud? Well, how have you all been this long time?"

"O you can see we are all well. How is Aunt Peggy?" said Helen."

"Well, Peggy is tolerable, she has a leetel touch of the rheumatiz, but she keeps a gwine and gets about right peart. She says you must all come over Saturday and take dinner with us, and bring your knittin' and spend the day. I must go up to Clarksville this mornin', but I rid by to light a minute. But I must be a gwine. Good mornin'." And the old man and old Ball were soon out of sight.

On Saturday Capt. Lawson and his family went

over to spend the day. What delightful times those all-day visits were. The motherly Aunt Peggy met them at the gate and kissed Mrs. Lawson and Helen tenderly and led them into the homely dwelling. I suppose it will change—indeed, I know it has changed—but I wish it never had, those days of old when wealth and style and culture did not come in to separate people who were made to love each other. I don't know enough about the way women entertain each other to tell of how pleasantly the hours passed by with Mrs. Lawson and Aunt Peggy, but this visit had an influence on Helen's future which was greater than she knew.

"Well, how my little gal has growed," said Aunt Peggy. "So you've left school, is you? and you can play the pianny and paint picters, but have you larned how to cook? Can ye cut and make your own frocks and make your pappy's coat and breeches?"

"Why no, Aunt Peggy, that was not taught at Dr. Marks's school."

"Well, it ought to have been. I tell you good vittals is a mighty helpful thing in this world, and you never know what's gwine to happen. Jeems won't let me cook now; but for ten year arter we was married he never eat a bite I did not cook, and I've larned Maria how to do it to suit him. You may never have it to do, your mother never has, but you don't know what'll come to pass."

"You are right, Aunt Peggy," said Mrs. Lawson. "I am only sorry I never did learn to do these things, and I wish Helen did know how to manage like you do."

"I tell you, Helen, my child, thar is nothin' mean about work; I know you can 'broider and do—what do you call that kind of knittin' you do with one needle?—crochshay, yes, but to make good butter, to cook good bread, to know how to manage with chickens which has the pip and the sore head (I never could manage coleray, though), is better than all that. Never, gal, put yourself whar you are obleeged to marry a rich man."

"Thank you, Aunt Peggy. If Aunt Judy don't drive me out of the kitchen, I am going to learn how to cook this summer."

When Roger went with the Squire and his father to the stable he asked for Jimmy.

"Jeems is down in the bottom. That young corn is growing mighty peart and needs plowing mighty bad, and he and the boys are at work thar. He'll be up to dinner, and he'll knock off then. I tell you, Captain, I believe in boys as havin' somethin' to do. The best thing for a boy like Roger here and Jeems is to have regular work. They must bar the yoke in their youth as the Scripter says. They think their daddies is right tight on 'em, but they get whar they know its best. Jeems would have liked to have rested to-day, case he thinks a power of Roger and Helen, but he said he would not do so. So, Roger, you must enjoy yourself as best you kin till he comes. You can take Trip and go a squirrelen or you can ride with me and your pappy over the farm."

"I'll take Trip and go squirreling," said Roger.

The Captain and the old man were riding along when the Squire said: "What's this about the Dimocrat party a splitten. What's it a splitten about anyhow?"

"Well, I don't know the cause of the split, but I fear the result of it."

"Do you think them black Republicans is got any chance to elect a President."

"Well, I am afraid they have a good one. I got a long letter from Alex Stephens (you know he and I were in college together), and he is much troubled."

"Well, you know, Captain, I am a Union Dimocrat. I voted for Andrew Jackson the first time I ever voted, but I've been afeared between the abolitioners and the fire eaters we was gwine to get into trouble." How is craps with you all?"

"Well, you know I've lost two crops of rice in succession, but the prospect now is good if we don't have another flood."

"How many niggers do you have to feed anyhow?"

"I have two hundred and fifty, all told, and when my rice fails it is an almost total failure. I have had to borrow money largely or sell my negroes, and I could not do that; but if I've a good crop this year, I hope I'll come out."

"Captain, what are you gwine to do with my boy Roger."

"Well, I am sending him to school, and he is about ready to enter the university. I want him to make a scholar. After that I will let him choose what to do."

"Captain, you and I have always been good friends, and, if you will allow me, I would like to say a few words, case I think you'll take it right."

"Certainly, only don't try to get me to go to class meeting again. I tried that once."

"Well, I ain't a gwine to do that; its about Roger. You are not settin' the right example before that boy."

The Captain's cheek reddened. "How," he said, "am I failing?"

"Well, when I tuck dinner with you last year you know right before Roger you asked me to jine you in a dram; and when I would not you tuck one yourself, and then you had wine on the table and Roger drunk a glass and you drunk two.

"Why certainly, I was raised that way and I never was drunk; and I want Roger to learn to control himself, so I never refuse him wine when he wants it."

"Well, Captain, I can't argy with you, but somehow it don't seem to me to be right. I am afeard of consequences. But thar's the dinner horn; let's go back."

Jimmy returned from the field and Roger from the wood, and the young plowman soon came from his room neatly clad in his Sunday suit. The Squire would not wear store clothes himself, but he bought them for Jeems he said; and as Jimmy had spent two years in his brother's counting-room in Atlanta, he had taken on the easy ways of a city boy, and when he welcomed Roger and Helen he did so with easy grace and greeted the fair girl with great heartiness, though his cheek reddened a little as he met her. The contrast between the sturdy form and high color of the mountain boy and the beautiful brunette from the coast was striking, and was not less a contrast than his hearty tone and open manner and her indescribable gentleness and sweetness of tone which marked the women of her class of coast people. Roger was delighted to see his old friend. Jimmy had been his earliest Habersham friend. They had fished for trout and perch and hunted birds and squirrels and had driven cattle for the Squire from the mountains together. Jimmy was was four years older than Roger, and the Captain and Mrs. Lawson were not unwilling for Roger to have a companion whom they could trust so implicitly. As for Helen, it was not to be supposed by them that she would feel anything greater than a friend's interest in Jimmy, nor did they suppose he would in her, and they were right. The old Squire and his good wife would have been as little pleased with the prospect of a tender passage between these young folks as the Captain and Mrs. Lawson. So if you think I am going to tell you a love story and to tell you that the handsome young plowman was going to fall in love with the planter's daughter, and that there was going to be a real romance, you are mistaken. The truth is, Mary Blakely, over the mountains, had already won Jimmy's heart, and at the last Loudsville camp meeting the engagement had been made, and that fact was much to the gratification of the old people, but that was no reason why Jimmy should not like Helen. She was as cordial as a warm-hearted girl could be, and he did like her. So when dinner was over the young folks went out hunting flowers on the hillsides, which only a month before had been bleak and bare. The mountain country where the Lawsons lived was over 1,800 feet higher than their coast plantation; and while the early flowers were gone long ago in Liberty, the fields and woods of Habersham were in richest loveliness in June.

It was late in the afternoon when, after a day of real enjoyment, the family returned home. The maid met them with the announcement that Col. Du Barry, his wife, and Miss Flora had called while they were gone, and left their cards and an invitation for them to dine at the "Crow's Nest" on Wednesday next.

Col. Du Barry was a retired factor from Savannah. He had a large planting interest in lower Georgia, several rice plantations, and any quantity of money and bonds. He did not like the watering places of the North, and his hay fever was relieved by the mountain air; and so he had an elegant home to which he came every year, and to which his wife came when she did not go to Saratoga or the White Sulphur, which she was pretty apt to do every summer. They were now in Habersham; and as they knew the Lawsons well, they called to invite them to dine. The invited guests went to the elegant dinner and had an evening of what the world calls enjoyment. The old Colonel and Mrs. Du Barry, and Capt. Lawson and Mrs. Lawson played whist at one table, and young Du Barry and his sister and Helen and Roger played another game of cards at another table. Wine was freely served at dinner, and all drank as a matter of course; but when they went home they agreed with Roger when he said: "You may say what you please, but I like Squire Bass and Aunt Peggy's plain ways better than all this fuss and feathers." That is, I am sure, the honest opinion we all have; but I fear that if you and I were rich enough we would rather be called Du Barry than Bass, and dine as late and in as good form as the Du Barrys did than at twelve o'clock and in the simple way of the Squire, but it would not make Roger's remark any the less sensible.

CHAPTER IV.

A CHAPTER WHICH I WISH COULD BE LEFT OUT.

THE love I had for Roger would have led me to have kept back everything which detracted from him, but a faithful biographer must tell the truth or not speak at all. Roger had been a good boy up to the present time. When he was very small he had been very religious. His old colored mammy used to talk to him a great deal about God and heaven and hell; and his dear mother used to read to him from the Bible and from good books, and teach him to sing and to pray. He learned the Shorter Catechism by heart, and old Dr. Preston, the pastor of Medway, after he was fourteen more than once expressed the hope that he would come into the Church at the next communion. It would have been so easy then for a gentle hand to have led him into the fold, for he was so near the kingdom of God; but childhood passed, and thoughtless boyhood came; and now he was nearing young manhood, and had not professed religion. He had been taught to shrink from falsehood, cowardice, penuriousness, rudeness, and

A REGRETFUL CHAPTER. 51

cruelty, and he had a wholesome aversion to them all; but alas! he had never been taught that religious faith was for a little boy, and he had not taken Jesus as his Saviour, and had never been made anew by his grace.

Dick Du Barry was as graceless a young reprobate as ever wore decent clothing, but he was as fascinating as he was vile. His mother was a woman of fashion, and his father a man of the world. The family was of the earth, earthy. Dick, although he was no orphan, had never known a mother's tender care. Another breast nourished him when a babe, and another hand attended him as a little child. High-spirited and willful, the handsome, smart little fellow soon learned how to tyrannize over inferiors and how to secure his ends, and he used his knowledge to good effect. His governess gave him up as incorrigible as she gave up her place, and he was sent while still a child to a boarding school, and sent back home by the teacher. Then, when he was older, he was sent to Maj. Bingham. The Major would have conquered the stubborn, willful boy by his military discipline; but he smuggled out a letter to his mother, telling the most doleful story of his wrongs, and she sent for him to come home. Then his father, who had been educated by the

Jesuits, sent him to Spring Hill; but the good fathers dismissed him from school, and he was now in Habersham.

There were some things Dick knew perfectly. He was fully up on etiquette, he knew how to dance all the new figures, and there was no game of cards, from faro to whist, which he could not teach one to play. He was a capital rider, a good shot, and dressed in perfect taste. There was nothing rude or blustering in his manner, and his French blood indicated its presence by a beautiful polish. He had seen the world; he had gone with his mother, season after season, to Saratoga and White Sulphur, in Virginia, and he went with her on her trip to Paris. He profited by his opportunities to learn everything that he ought not to have known.

Poor Roger was never away from his country home. Unsuspecting, confiding, he was just such a boy as nearly always falls a victim to such a foe as young Du Barry was.

Dick did not dislike Roger; on the other hand, he was very fond of him, and it was all the worse for Roger that he was. In a little while Roger was completely under his control, and woe to him that it was so! Every day they were together.

In Dick's bedroom there was a trunk in which

he had stored away a number of those vile books which even the law shuts out from the mails, and whose only claim to distinction is that they are vile. He had no end of stories of flirtations and escapades. Many of these stories were false, and some, alas! were true.

The young folks at "Crow's Nest" and "Ivy Bush" had their card parties and their dances and their excursions; the heads of the families still opened their wine, and drank their cognac. The Lawson family went in regularly to the little church in the village, and Mrs. Lawson read devoutly her Bible every day, and read the *New York Observer* on Sunday afternoon; and no one saw that a serpent was already coiled, and about to strike the son, the pride of the household.

It was by gradual, and yet rapid, movement that the noble boy fell into bad ways. I need not particularize. He was but a boy, not quite seventeen, a warm-hearted, thoughtless, fun-loving boy, without religion, who had been allowed to tamper with drink and with cards all his life. He knew that his mother would never suspect him of wrongdoing, and believed that his father would not be severe in his censure of his vagaries if he should discover them. When he first became conscious that he had taken too much wine, there was a feeling of deep shame and remorse; but the pride of the Lawsons came to his aid, and he resolved that he would prove he was strong enough to resist the next time. True, Dick Du Barry had taken three glasses to his one, but he would not go even that far again, even though he did not totally abstain.

Dick and Roger were almost inseparable. His old friend, Jimmie Bass, found Roger somewhat cold, and quietly drew off from him; and the Squire looked sad when Roger's name was mentioned, and when Dick and Roger came dashing by old Ball and his master as they were going to Clarksville, and there was scarcely a recognition, the old man's face was shadowed, and he said to himself, " Tut, tut! shame, shame! blind, blind!" What he meant he knew. I could only conjecture.

The billiard room in Clarksville was a favorite resort of the boys, and Roger and Dick joined their other friends. The pool was made, money was lost and won in trifling amounts; but gaming had begun.

The Captain was absorbed in politics; Helen was painting a landscape and reading Mr. Dickens's new book, " Dombey and Son; " and poor Roger was going to the bad, and nobody saw it. Nobody? Yes, One saw it, and that One in mercy interfered.

His divine Father had an eye on him which never slept, and he is understood how to act. There are times that sin has to uncover itself and show what it will do before the sinner will pause; but the devil sometimes defeats himself, or his agents disobey his instructions.

Dick and Roger, often under the pretense of going to churches to meeting, took long rides into the country round about; and though they did go to meeting, they went for a frolic, and not for devotion.

One Saturday Dick said to Roger: "Roger, there's going to be a meeting of the Tiger Tail Association up on Tallulah to-morrow, and a crowd of us are going up to have a rare time. Don't let the women folks know where you are going, but just tell them you are going to church, and ride over by my house and we'll go up."

"All right; I'll come."

Roger did not come to that conclusion without compunction, but he had committed himself to Dick so completely that he was not disposed to resist. Dick and the Heyward boys and Alfred Hartley formed a group of fast low-country boys, all older than Roger and all of them from the best families. They hunted deer and foxes together, and in all the frolics of the time they had their share. They did not always go to the most reputable places and did not meet the most reputable people, and sometimes they had unpleasant conflicts with the county youths.

The Durham boys lived in a cove of the mountains. There were five of them. They were rude, uneducated, coarse, and courageous. They delighted in their physical strength and enjoyed nothing more than a row. The *coterie* of low-country bloods had aroused their ire, and there was danger of open conflict. It came sooner than they thought. The young men from the low country who went to the Association were all drinking, Roger among them. They were in a hilarious mood when they reached the grounds where the Association was held. There was quite a crowd gathered. A shelter was made by placing the boughs of the small oaks on a frame, and seats were made of logs. This constituted the preaching place. The preachers, dressed in homely garb, were preaching from this stand. Elder Pigeon, from Rabun, was holding forth in a quaint style on "And the oil stayed;" and he was followed by Elder Tucker, on "And he took thereout a rib." The sermons were certainly unique enough, and the tone was as striking as the texts were odd. The group of which Roger was one were more amused than profited, and they did not hide their merriment. More than once they laughed outright. Bob Durham was not a member of the old side Church, but he was akin to the preacher who was forced to rebuke sharply the irreverent youngsters, and his ire rose at their disrespect to the place. He glared at the crowd angrily, and when they rose to leave, as they did in the midst of the sermon, he and his brothers rose too, and they went to where the offenders had their horses. Walking up to Dick Du Barry, he said sharply: "Well, you'd better leave here. You think yourself powerful smart with your fine clothes and highty-tighty airs, but if you don't leave here pretty quick there'll be a way found to make ye."

The boys were half intoxicated and were ready for a row. Dick was no coward; and, shaking his whip at Durham, he angrily said: "You'll make me, will you? If you don't want a taste of this whip, you will get away from here."

"I will, will I? If you'll pull off that broadcloth coat and stand up like a man, I'll teach you some manners."

"Manners, you blackguard? You'll teach me? I'll horsewhip you if you say a word."

"Well, maybe you will, smarty, after I've

smacked your jaws, and I'll do that before you know it."

With a sudden stroke Dick brought his whip down on the rustic's shoulders, and in a moment the sturdy mountaineer had him by the throat and blow after blow from the stout hickory riding switch he had in his hand fell on the broadcloth coat of Du Barry.

Roger rushed up to the aid of his friend, and Bill Durham, Bob's sturdy brother, seized him and threw him down; and was about to fall upon him when Jim Phillips and Jimmy Bass came on the scene. Phillips separated the two combatants, Du Barry and Bob; and Jimmy seized Roger and violently led him away.

"That will do, Bob," said Phillips; "let him alone; I'll take care of him."

"Well, take him away, Jim Phillips. You's a gentleman, if you is rich; but if you don't, I'll maul the life outen him."

Roger was angry enough to have dared any danger, and struggled to rush to his friend's help; but he was a child in Jimmy's hands, and Jimmy held him firmly as he said to Bill: "Bill, you and I are good friends; now let this drop for my sake."

"Well, Jim, I will, but no man shall tech my brother in a far fight."

The feeling of Roger as he rode away was not to be envied; the Sabbath desecrated, and now a disgraceful row in which he bore so shameful a part was what his course brought about, and his mortification and anger were both increased when the very person who had influenced him to do these things angrily said: "Roger Lawson, you are a brave friend, aren't you, to stand by and see a friend beaten like a dog because you were too cowardly to help him?"

"He did want to help you, Mr. Du Barry," said Jimmy Bass very decidedly; "and if there is anybody to blame for his not doing it, it is not Roger Lawson but Jimmy Bass, and you know where to find him."

Jimmy and Roger rode on together. The others of the group had now come up; and Du Barry, angry and humiliated, rode off at a rapid pace with them.

"Roger," said Jimmy, as they parted at the gate, "I'll see you to-morrow night. Good-bye now."

The next night he came, and Roger joined him for a walk. "Roger," said his old friend, "we've been boys together, and I've seen where you were going to lately, and now this thing must be stopped, or you are a ruined boy. To think of your mother's son and Miss Helen's brother taking up with such a crowd! I am ashamed of you."

Roger's eyes were opened. He saw the gulf he had just escaped, and not too soon; but the deepest pang was before him. His father, ignorant of what had happened, went to the village, when Col. Billups called him into his office. "Captain," he said, "Squire Larkins came to see me to-day to have a presentment made to the next grand jury of a crowd of boys who are accused of disturbing public worship, and your boy was among them. I begged the Squire to hold up till I could see you."

"Impossible! Col. Billups, it is impossible! My boy has been too well bred."

"Well, you see Jimmy Bass. He was there, and will tell you all about it."

He went at once to the Squire's, and sent for Jimmy. Jimmy told the story as it was. Roger was intoxicated, and he did disturb public worship.

The Captain's face burned with indignation. "To think that I have trusted him so, and he has disgraced me! I will send him to Maj. Bingham, and let him tame him," he said to Squire Bass.

Squire Bass said calmly and gently, but sadly:

A REGRETFUL CHAPTER.

"No, Captain, you will do no sich thing. You remember my talk with you. You are to blame, not the boy."

"Yes, Squire, I am. It Roger goes to the bad, I am to blame; but hear me, the last decanter of brandy has been used at my house, and the last bottle of wine has been opened there."

"That's right, Captain. Now don't be hard on Roger. I've raised six boys. I know 'em. Take the self-respect from 'em, and you haint nothin' left. Talk plain to him, but be kind. Make him quit a goin' with that Du Barry boy. Give him somethin' to do, and trust in God for the rest."

"Thank you, my old friend; and may God forgive a poor, misguided, sinning father, and save his boy from ruin!"

The Captain came sadly home. He saw that the frank face of his proud boy was clouded, and the firm-set lips told of his determination to resent rebuke, but rebuke did not come. The father told his son sadly of what he had heard, told him of the pang he had suffered, and then made an honest and humble confession of his own error. The boy was melted. He asked his father not to let his mother or Helen know; and they never did, and so Roger escaped the snare.

CHAPTER V.

SOME PLEASING EVENTS.

HELEN had not forgotten the advice given by Aunt Peggy, and she had intended to act upon it; but she had delayed, partly because she had a picture to finish, and partly because she was afraid of Mom Judy. Mom Judy, the widow of Daddy Juba, had been the chief cook of the Lawsons ever since Helen could remember, and no Catherine of Russia, or Elizabeth of England, ever ruled with a more autocratic sway than Mom Judy ruled her kitchen. She was almost as broad as she was long. Her head was always turbaned with a red handkerchief, and her strong arms were bare to the elbow. Her kitchen was her castle, and no one dared to cross its sacred threshold without her consent. She had a helper in a negro girl, whom she could alternately lecture, advise, and scold; but for this I cannot say what would have become of Mom Judy. I hope, however, the effect of Chloe's absence would not have been quite so serious as she said: "De trute is, honey,

I am jes obleeged to scole somebody, or dis ole nigger would bust wide open; she would for true." And that would have been a calamity of no small magnitude. She came every morning to her mistress to get orders for the day, and Helen went with her to the pantry and the smokehouse, and supplied her demands, and after these stores went into the kitchen no one knew more of them till they reappeared on the table.

The kitchen was some little distance from the house. It was a rather large room with a large fireplace, in which was a crane for the pot, and a full supply of pots, kettles, ovens, skillets, spiders, frying pans, etc., and, indeed, all the needful furniture for a good kitchen.

The floor was always neatly sanded with white sand from the brook, and the room was kept scrupulously clean.

Stoves were not common in the South in that day; and while there was one here, Mom Judy protested against the innovation, and still used her old utensils. Indeed, if she could not have seen the red coals on the lid and basted the big turkey in the great oven and heard the bubbling of the boiling pot, she would have been unhappy.

Chloe was her scullion. She was her granddaughter, and Mom Judy's ambition was to make a high-order cook out of Chloe; but the wayward girl taxed her patience sorely. To-day, as usual, Mom Judy was on the rampage, and Chloe was in vain protesting, with an air of injured innocence, in a kind of soliloquy: "I clar I cain't please grandmammy no way; if I does somethin' she fusses, if I does nothin' she fusses, if I try to please her she fusses, and if I don't try to please her she fusses; she is de worry ob my life."

She was now giving Chloe fair warning that she "would bust her head open wid dat rollin' pin de fust thing she knowed," which threats did not seem to alarm Chloe in the least.

Just then Helen came tripping into the kitchen. In a moment there was a calm, and a broad smile covered the black face as she said: "Well, little missie, glad to see you in de kitchen. What kin your old mammy do fer you?"

"Well, Aunt Judy, I have come to get you to learn me to cook."

An expression of blank amazement came over the old face. Was her "little missie jes a projeckin' wid her. Yes, dat was it," and with a hearty laugh she said: "I larn you to cook? Yes, when my little missie larns ole Judy how to play de peanner."

"No, Aunt Judy, I am serious; I want to learn how to cook."

Aunt Judy looked in alarm. Had her little mistress lost her mind? What was the matter? But Helen said: "Now, Aunt Judy, be a good old dear, and show me how. Aunt Peggy told me to learn."

"Well, dat splains it. When quality folks go wid buckra folks deys gwine to larn buckra ways. Why, little missus, dat ting jes can't be. I been cook for my ole missus, your mudder's mudder, an' my young missus, your mudder, an' nebber one er dem put de foot in de kitchen, 'cept to give me my orders. Why, little missie, it jes cain't be."

"But, Aunt Judy, we may be poor some day."

"Po? Why, Miss Helen! Who eber hear ob a Lawson er a Maxwell bein' po? Ain't massa got two hundred an' fifty likely niggers, an' eber so many tousand acres er land? an' now you want to cook like po buckra. No, little missie, it jes cain't be."

"But I may marry a poor man, and have to work some day."

"You marry a po man? You—what, Col. Maxwell's granddarter? Why, Miss Helen, a po man won't dar look at you. No, you go back an' paint your pretty pictures; you cain't come in here."

"Well, Aunt Judy, mother says I may."

"Well, ef young missus say so, den I say so. Now, dar's dat new ting over dar yer pappy brougnt nere, dat new stove. I ain't use 'em, and I don't want to use 'em; but I'll make Chloe kindle you a fire in 'em, and den I'll do what young missie say. But what would my ole missus say if she seed it?"

So Helen took her first lesson in the fine art of cooking.

I confess my ignorance along here. The mysteries of the kitchen I reckon I will never solve; but my admiration for the girl who knows how to broil a steak, make a roll, or draw a cup of rich, clear coffee from the fragrant berry, grows with my advancing years.

When Roger saw his sister in the kitchen he resolved that he would learn something too. He proposed to his father to take a farm hand's place for the summer, and the Captain employed him at regular wages; and he donned the dress of a farmer boy, and went into the field regularly. What he did, he did well. Jimmy Bass and he met in the hayfields and the cornfields. Dick Du Barry no longer recognized him, and Miss Flora only nodded her head; but Roger cared little for that. He had more serious views of life, and took up again those religious habits which he for some time past had laid aside, and was Roger over again.

CHAPTER VI.

A RATHER DULL BUT AN IMPORTANT CHAPTER.

CAPT. LAWSON was quite an intelligent man, and took great interest in political matters. He saw the clouds gathering in deeper volume on the political sky, and could not conceal his anxiety. Few persons at this day can realize the bitterness of the political parties before the war. There were then in the field four parties: the Breckinridge Democrat, the Douglas Democrat, the Bell and Everett or American party, and the Republicans. The Republican party had no existence in Georgia, and so bitter was the feeling against it that one's life would have been in danger if he had avowed connection with that party. Two things had fastened themselves on every Southern mind: the one that if negro slavery was overthrown white men could not live in the South; and the other, that the Republican party was determined to overthrow it. The first of these views was not correct, we know, but it was held; and the last may not have been true, and was certainly disavowed. It was hoped by men like Capt. Lawson that the middle ground of the American party, as unobjectionable, and men as John Bell and Edward Everett, who were candidates, might be accepted by both sections and that peace might still hold sway, but it was soon evident that when a divided Democratic and a united Republican party were in conflict there could be but one result, and from that Capt. Lawson shrank back in great dread. He had returned with his family to Liberty. The rice had been reaped and thrashed and sent to his factors in Savannah to be prepared for market; for after the grain has been cleared from straw and chaff on the plantation it must be pounded at the rice mills in the city until the yellow covering is stripped from it, when it is sorted and packed in tierces, and shipped to all parts of the world. There had no disaster befallen the crop, and all things on the estate promised well. The Captain cast his ballot for John Bell and Edward Everett and went to his home. He had a feeling of genuine depression, for he felt assured that his vote had been in vain, and it was. In a week came the news. The Republican party was victorious. Mr. Lincoln was elected. There was now consternation throughout the South. Something must be done, but what? I have a vivid remembrance of these days,

DULL BUT IMPORTANT. 69

and one more vivid than pleasant. When the Captain reached home the cloud on his face told of the news he had heard.

"Well, my dear," said his wife, "what is the matter?"

"As I feared, Mr. Lincoln is elected, and what that means God only can tell."

"Well, what of that? Surely the election of a candidate you did not prefer does not mean so much as you seem to think."

"No, it would not if it had been Douglas or Breckinridge. But a black Republican in the Presidency will not be borne. He must be a foe to slavery, and its overthrow is our ruin. South Carolina will secede, and other slave States will follow."

"Will there be a war?"

"God forbid! Alex Stephens writes me, however, that if there is secession it will certainly come; and when it comes who can tell what will be the end? Alas for party hate!"

That night Roger and his father had a long talk. If my young friends will be a little patient, perhaps I can tell them what they have wished to know: why so many good people in the South went into the war.

"Father," said Roger, "who made the Union?"

"The colonies, my son."

"What colonies?"

"The thirteen independent colonies."

"Who made them independent?"

"The English Government, whose colonies they were, declared them such."

"How came these independent governments united into one."

"They made a Confederacy."

"For what purpose?"

"For their own protection."

"Did any one surrender all right to withdraw from this Confederacy?"

"No; on the contrary, some of them stipulated that they would withdraw if their safety demanded it."

"Did any State ever do so?"

"No."

"Did any ever propose to do so?"

"Yes; the New England States said that if certain things were not done they would withdraw."

"Were these things done?"

"They were, or at least the grievance was removed."

"Why are we afraid of Mr. Lincoln?"

"Because he is put in by the antislavery people."

"Will they destroy slavery?"

"They promise to do so."

"Will that destroy us?"

"It will."

"Can't we keep him out of his seat?"

"No; that would not be lawful."

"Can we secede or withdraw lawfully?"

"I think so."

"Peaceably?"

"I fear not.

"Father, are you a citizen of the United States?"

"No; I am a citizen of Georgia first, and then a citizen of the United States because I am a Georgian."

"If there should be a war, who must you obey?"

"My State."

"Well, I hope there won't be a war; but if it comes, I know who'll whip."

"Well, who?"

"The South; that's who."

"Don't be too certain. But it is not yet certain that we will be forced to these stern measures."

I should not, however, be a fair historian of these times if I led my young readers to think that the side which Capt. Lawson took was the only side that was taken in the South, and that all Southern people saw matters as he did. The fact was far otherwise. There were many excellent people in the South who believed, as nearly all the people of the North, that a State had no right to secede, and who looked upon all movements in that direction as treason. They were not lawless, not even abolitionists, and would not have done injustice to any, but they held to this opinion most strongly.

Old Dr. Prescott, the pastor of Medway, was a Connecticut man. He had been in the South many years, and was a bitter opponent of anti-slavery men or abolitionists. He said that he honestly believed the negro was better cared for as a slave than he would be as a freeman, and that neither the Bible nor the Constitution of the United States forbade slavery in some form; and he believed the abolitionist was a foe to the negro's best interest. Like Capt. Lawson, the old doctor was a conservative and voted for John Bell and Edward Everett. He came over to the Captain's a few days after the announcement of Mr. Lincoln's election, and naturally the question of "What now?" came up for discussion.

"Well, Doctor," said the Captain, "what is the prospect?"

"Gloomy, sir, gloomy."

"Will South Carolina secede?"

"I think she will."

"Has she a right to do so?"

"I think not."

"When did she surrender it?"

"When she accepted the present Constitution."

"Why, is not that a compact between the States?"

"No; it is a union of the people."

"Well, we will not discuss that point; but if she does secede, can the other States force her back?"

"I fear they will try."

"Then what?"

"Then God pity my poor country!" And the old doctor's lips quivered and the subject was changed.

CHAPTER VII.

THE WAR DRUM.

IF my young readers wish to get a true history of how the war commenced and of how it progressed and of how it ended, and will give a lifetime to its study, they may find the facts out, but they cannot get them from this chronicle. It has only to do with what Roger Lawson did in the war, and so this chronicler can tell only a part of the story.

The States seceded, the war began, troops were called for, and the Liberty Troop offered itself to the Governor for service, and was accepted.

Capt. Lawson, with his servant boy, young Jack, and his son Roger, joined the troop, which rendezvoused at Walthourville, and from thence went into camp to be drilled for service. The old Taylor Creek Camp Ground was chosen as the camp of instruction, and the tents made good barracks, and the old field near by good parade grounds. The month that was spent in the camp was a month of real jollity. Mrs. Lawson, Helen, and Roger came to remain while the troops were there. It had not been Capt. Lawson's intention to take Roger with him to the army; and while Roger was eager to go, he was not willing to ask his parents to permit him to do so, because he thought he ought not to leave his mother. But Mrs. Lawson could not consent for her husband to go without her son, and she insisted that Roger should go, which he did as his father's orderly.

There had never been a war in the memory of any of the Liberty County people, and all the soldiers they had ever seen had been merely holiday soldiers. There were perhaps none, North or South, who realized in 1861 what war meant. The horses were fat and well groomed, the uniforms were new and bright with their gold trappings. The shrill fife and drum and the cavalry bugle kept the camp alive. Wives and mothers and sweethearts came to the camp to visit the soldiers; the tables were spread with abundance of food, and in the balmy air of the Southern spring this life out of doors had a wondrous charm. But this kind of soldier life could not continue long. The first battle of Manassas came on while they were in camp, and the Troop was ordered to rendezvous at Atlanta, where it was to become a part of the First Battalion of Georgia Cavalry and elect its officers. Then the farewells were sadly spoken, and the bugle sounded and the troop began its march. When the battalion was organized in Atlanta Capt. Lawson was elected lieutenant colonel commanding; and then his command was ordered to report at Lynchburg, Va., where it would receive further orders.

The horses were put in the stock cars, and the men and officers in the freight cars, which were provided with rough seats, and they were conveyed by rail to Lynchburg. This charming city on the upper James was a delightful place for a rendezvous, and the handsome young fellows who composed the battalion had the *entrée* into the elegant society of the old town. And for several weeks while they were awaiting orders there was a round of festivities. But at last orders came to march. Col. Lawson was to report with his battalion to Brig. Gen. Floyd, at Sewell Mountains, W. Va. The brigade was to be transported by rail to Jackson's River, and thence march to Sewell. Roger's own account of his first campaign is, perhaps, as good as anything I can give. It was in a letter to Helen:

JACKSON'S RIVER, W. VA., September, 1861.

My Dear Helen: Well, we are here at last, and such a time we had to get here. It was jolly at Camp Brown, in Liberty; but that was nothing to Lynchburg. The city is built on the side of a steep hill, and when you are on the top of that one there is another hill yet. I think that a hogshead of tobacco would roll down a half-mile into the river without stopping if it got started on the hilltop. But such clever people and such pretty girls you never saw. The girls came in crowds to see our dress parades, and we had all our best uniforms out, and were on our best behavior, and we had a grand time. But the order came for us to move on. The gruff old quartermaster, when he saw our big trunks, told us that we had better store them there, for he would not try to get them over the mountains. So we left all our dress uniforms, and took our fatigue suits.

We had a pleasant enough time in getting to Charlottesville. It is only sixty miles from Lynchburg; but it took us all day to make the trip, and there we had to change to another railroad.

Charlottesville is a quaint old town, where the University of Virginia is located. We could see "Monticello," where Mr. Jefferson lived, from the town; but we could not go out to it. We started early in the morning for this place. I did not know till I got fairly started on this journey how little I knew of Virginia.

We were soon in the mountains, and passed through one tunnel a mile long. The scene at Rockfish Gap, just before we entered the tunnel, was the finest I ever saw. I cannot describe it; but I wish you could see it.

Our train moved very slowly, and when we reached Staunton, a nice little city famous for its schools, we were halted for the night. We got out of the cars, and kindled some camp fires and had some coffee, and spread our blankets on the grass and slept.

The next day we steamed away again, and it was not long before we were in the wildest country you ever saw. Mountains were on all sides of us. The railway crept along their sides, and when we reached Millboro we had to have two engines.

The country has grown wilder and wilder ever since we left Staunton, and at last when we reached here we were simply nowhere. We are at the jumping off place, you may be sure. There is nothing here but scenery; but there is plenty of that. I forgot, there is not only scenery, but beef; such beef I never saw before. Great steers, which must weigh nearly two thousand pounds, are here by the hundreds. We are going to leave to-morrow.

I am as well as I can be, and feel as happy as a boy can who has left his heart behind him, for I must tell you a secret: There was a pretty girl in Lynchburg named Kitty Payne, whom I used to go to see, and I feel mighty like a fellow with a Payne in his heart.

Give a hundred kisses to mamma, and tell Mom Judy I wish that she could see the biscuits that Jack makes. It would make her jump. We will use them in our light artillery when we get out of balls. Good-bye. ROGER.

Jackson's River, although it seemed a long way from civilization, was after all over fifty miles from the point they were aiming at. Gen. Floyd was at Sewell, and Gen. Rosecrans was in his front, and Gen. R. E. Lee was coming with the troops from Cheat Mountain to bring on an engagement. So there was but little time for waiting, and as soon as the troops were rested they moved forward; but Roger stopped long enough at the next camp to write to Helen:

WHITE SULPHUR SPRINGS, W. VA., September, 1861.

My Dear Helen: We wished to leave early in the morning for a long march, but by the time we got our baggage wagons, and our horses in proper shape, and our rations cooked papa said that we could not make more than ten miles. He told me that he had dispatches from Gen. Floyd not to push his men, and while he wasted no time to come on without hurry, so we started for Callahan's, where we were to camp.

I reckon you have heard of roads, but such a road as this turnpike is you never dreamed of. It has rained, and rained, and rained. The very bottom seems to have dropped out of the roads, and four horses can hardly haul four barrels of flour. Our horses go floundering through mud and mire, and we are spattered with mud from head to foot.

Covington is a pretty little town at the base of the mountains, with the Jackson River winding all around it; but we had no time to stop, and so over the mountains we pressed to where there is a gap or narrow passage between them. Here there is an old time tavern kept by an old Irishman named Callahan. If you remember, Porte Crayon, in *Harper*, told of this very place. We found a good camp in the meadow, and Jack made us some good coffee and broiled us some nice beef, and we had a good night's rest.

Some of the Liberty boys grumble about these mountains. You know some of them never saw anything higher than a gopher hill till they left with the troop; but generally they take it all in good humor. We had a long march over the mountains the next day. For five miles we never saw a house, and then for fifteen miles not another. One man, whose name is Sprauls (or Sprawls), lives out here by himself. He makes some corn. The boys say that he plants it by shooting the grains into the side of the mountain with a rifle, for they say it is too steep to plant it any other way.

Well, you have heard Flora Du Barry talk about the White. It surpasses her power to exaggerate, and you know that it is pretty good. It is the most beautiful spot I ever saw. Surrounded by mountains on all sides, with a great big hotel and a great many cottages, and a lawn that must have been charmingly beautiful before it was so neglected. Everything is now out of order, and the hotel and cottages are used for hospitals. There are a great many of our men sick. We have measles, and mumps, and fever; but I am thankful that papa and I keep well. I like the army. I don't know how I will like it if we have any fighting. Papa has just got a dispatch from Gen. Floyd, who says he must be at Meadow Bluff to-morrow night. So we will have a long march, and must start early.

Don't forget to kiss dear old mamma a hundred times for her boy, and tell Mammy howdy.

Gen. Lee was in charge of the Western Virginia Department, and the Confederacy was attempting the foolish task of holding the western part of Virginia to the Southern Confederacy by sending its best troops and most accomplished commanders to that field. Gen. Lee had decided to make a movement by which he hoped to draw the wily Rosecrans into a battle. He had ordered Gen. Floyd to the summit of Little Sewell Mountain, and he now moved with his troops from Camp Alleghany to join him. Col. Lawson's battalion and a regiment of Georgia infantry were ordered to report to Gen. Floyd. The difficulty of supplying these troops so far from the base of supplies was very great, and horses and men had scant enough fare. The battalion left the White for the army at early dawn the day after Roger wrote. They had no breakfast, and made their first halt at Lewisburg. Roger, as soon as he reached Lewisburg, wrote, this time to his mother:

LEWISBURG, W. VA., September 10, 1861.

My Dear Mother: I wrote Helen from White Sulphur. Beautiful as the White was, we were glad to leave there. What our horses could not find in the meadows around they had to go without. Poor little Daisy looked so wan and I was so sorry for her that I gave her the bread which Jack gave me for my breakfast. We had a muddy road. We passed out of the valley, and just between the mountains a crystal stream, now full because of the heavy rains, was roaring away on our left, and a high mountain covered with yew trees and white pines and laurels was on the right. There were no settlements till we reached the Greenbrier River. We crossed on a bridge, and then such a climb as we had over the river hills. Our battalion could not keep up any order, for the long train of provision wagons was before us, and we had to move like snails. You may imagine we wanted our breakfast before we got it, but after a tiresome march we pitched our camp on a hill in the village of Lewisburg. This is a little village, which seems to be a very nice place. When we pitched our camp and while we were getting forage for our horses and breakfast for ourselves we had a chance to see some of the girls of the village. If I had not lost my heart in Lynchburg, I think one of these Lewisburg girls would have captured me. Well, we had to wait here for our wagon train till after dinner. A gentleman named Montgomery came to camp and asked to see papa, and told him that some of the men had been burning his rails. He told papa that he had plenty of wood that was at the service of the troops, and asked him to order the men to use that and not destroy his fences. Papa sent an orderly quick and stopped the men; and then Mr. Montgomery asked us to take dinner with him, and we went. He has such a nice home and such sweet little children. He is a good Presbyterian, too. They say the people in this western part of Virginia are all Union folks, but I don't think they are; all these Lewisburg people are very strong Southerners. Well, we got away at last; and leaving a few sick here, we marched on toward the Meadows. Gen. Lee came down to-day, and I saw him and his staff. He is a very elegant soldier with a gray mustache and no whiskers. He had on a very plain, neat suit of blue and rode a beautiful white horse which he bought here in Lewisburg. Papa came to see him, and he shook hands with him very cordially, as he did with me. His adjutant brought us orders to remain and bring up the rear guard to-morrow. I am having a good time. Don't be worried about me. Papa is quite well. I will write to Helen from our next stopping place, which will be I don't know where; but papa says Meadow Bluff, where Gen. Wise's brigade is.

Roger had now begun to know some of the hardships of camp life. It was a very different thing from what he had supposed it would be. I am sure from my experience in camp that the one who went a soldiering to have a good time was badly cheated. The cavalry went splashing through the mud in the middle of the turnpike, and the infantry walked through the fields and wherever they could find ground dry enough to walk on. Rains fell almost every day, as if the heavens were weeping over the fratricidal strife. The men were going they knew not where, and everything looked dreary. The bright-hearted Roger, however, kept up his spirits and the spirits of those around him; and wrote cheerfully to his mother when the weary march ended for a while at Little Sewell:

LITTLE SEWELL, September, 1861.

My Precious Mother: Well, we are here at last! When we reached Jackson's River I wrote Helen that we had reached the jumping off place, but we have now jumped clear off. We are in the woods on a mountain with not an inhabited house in—I don't know how far. I did not know there was so wild a spot in all Virginia, and O what a time we had in getting to it. We left everything that we could leave in Lewisburg, and began our march for this camp. For five miles we had a beautiful country to march through. The hills were covered with blue grass, and on every farm were fine brick residences. The heavy wagon trains had worn the pike into holes and ruts, and the troops have swept the farms clean of everything like fences, and chickens and ducks I fear have fared badly, for I am sorry to say the average soldier don't think it a sin to steal a chicken; and as Jack had a little inclination that way before he entered the army, I fear he has not improved. I am afraid the chicken pie he served to-day for dinner did not come from a bought fowl. Andy Rhodes, one of papa's men, from Cherokee, said: "Yes he did kill the ducks, and he intended to kill every duck which tried to bite him." Well, we had a great time sleeping out without tents in the rain, but we got along very well. We made a great big fire and stretched a pole over some forks and then put up some rails on that and covered that frame with our oilcloths, and then we laid some rails close together and put some hay on them and then our blankets on that, and laid down, clothes, boots, and all, and slept O how sweetly.

I have not heard from you since I was at Lynchburg. You asked me if I went to church. O yes, I did; and I went to the Methodist Church because—well, you know Miss Kitty went there, and her father had a pew, and she asked me to go with her; but papa went to hear Dr. Hoge, the Presbyterian. No; I have not touched wine or cards or whisky, and I don't intend to. Dont be bothered about us and don't be scared about the battle which we look for every day. If old "Rosey" tries to come up this hill, we are ready for him. Our cavalry are having a right hard time scouting and going on picket, but the infantry say the cavalry are just scaring up the bears for them to fight while they get away; but you know that isn't so.

Give Helen and Mammy my love. And be sure and write a long letter to me and papa, at Lewisburg. Direct to us " Lewisburg Army, West Va., Lawson's Battalion, Georgia Cavalry," and we'll get the letter.

Affectionately, ROGER.

Col. Lawson added a P. S.:

Roger has left his letter open for me to finish. You need not fear an engagement. I saw Gen. Floyd to-day, and we together saw Gen. Lee. He says he does not think that Rosecrans is going to move on us, and he evidently does not expect to move on him; and I see all things are ready to go back to Camp Alleghany. I am so glad that I brought Roger with me. He makes a fine soldier. He did not write you about a little incident that touched me very much. As we rode over toward Sewell from Meadow Bluff I noticed a poor infantry soldier who had fallen out. He was completely exhausted. Roger rode up to where he was, and got off his horse, and helped the poor fellow to mount, and walked beside Daisy till they reached a house by the wayside. He went in and got the people to take the poor fellow in. Roger had walked five miles.

We are having rather wet weather; but don't be uneasy about us.

Roger wrote to Helen two days after:

SEWELL, September, 1861.

Dear Helen: Well, old " Roscy " is gone. We woke up yesterday morning, and found that his white tents were no longer to be seen, and Gen. Floyd ordered papa to send a company as a scouting party to see what had become of him. So papa sent the troop, and of course I went. We went on an old road which used to be here before the turnpike was made, and went cautiously till we were in full sight of the retreating army. We could see them from the place where we stood, and saw that they had left Big Sewell sure enough. Why, I don't know. There seemed to be a great army of them; but they have vamoosed, and after all our marching and all the mud, we did not fire a gun except at some sheep; but we did fire at them, and killed them too. You see rations run mighty short, and somebody told Capt. Rich that he saw a flock of sheep; and papa asked Gen. Floyd if he might capture them and use them for the men. He told him yes, but told him to be sure and order his men not to shoot. They found the sheep, and took after them; but the sheep were running too fast for them, and Andy Rhodes, the man the ducks were about to bite, could not stand it, so he let loose with his navy, and got a sheep every fire.

When we heard the shots we supposed that the battle was on, and the men went to the breastworks; but no enemy came. They sent one of the sheep to old Gen. Floyd, and he forgave the shooting; for no one knew who shot, so they said, after the officer began to inquire about it.

We are still going westward—where, I don't know; and nobody else does but Gen. Floyd. Gen. Lee and his troops have gone back, and we march to-morrow. ROGER.

CHAPTER VIII.

HELEN.

I MUST not forget Mrs. Lawson and Helen. While Roger was undergoing the hardships of the campaign the good folks at home were not without their cares. It was impossible for them to go to Habersham, and it was not at all safe for them to stay on the plantation during the fall. Capt. Lawson had been called away so suddenly that he had been compelled to leave the selection of a summer home to his wife. Helen was a gentle and very quiet but a very decided person, and she realized that her tender mother was not able to cope with the trials before her. She saw that this question about a home must be settled. So she rode over on her pony to Mr. William Jones, the overseer, to have a consultation. He was at home on the veranda smoking his after dinner pipe when she came in. Putting the pipe aside and hastily drawing on his homespun coat, he met her at the steps, and politely placed a chair for her, and waited for her to begin the conversation.

After meeting the overseer's wife and looking

at the baby, the young mistress of the plantation seated herself and began to open her plans.

"You know, Mr. Jones, we must get away from here soon, and we cannot go to 'Ivy Bush' this summer, and I've come over to see you about what we are to do."

"Well, Miss Helen, I've been a considerin' of that myself; but I'm afeared my plans won't exactly suit you."

"Well, what are they?"

"Well, I don't think this war is gwine to be a short un, and I hain't mighty sure which side is gwine to be on top when it's over, and my erpinion is that the best way to do is to 'take time by the forelock,' as my daddy used to say, and my own idee is to buy a piney woods place away from the coast, and move some of the stock and all of the sheep up thar; and that will be a place whar Mrs. Lawson and you can summer. It may be a leetle lonesome; but I think I can get a place in a good settlement, and you will have good neighbors, if they is plain."

"Mr. Jones, do you know a place like that?"

"Yes, I think I do. Billy McCord had two lots up near John's, jest ajining, and he's gone to the war, and his wife wants to go over to Tattnall to stay with her married darter; and I heard that he wanted to sell out and buy over thar."

"What do you think the place would cost?"

"Well, the land hain't fust-class, though when it's trod and well worked it makes good truck; but it's a powerful healthy, and I think Miss McCord will sell cheap. I have heard that she would take $3,000 for the whole thing."

"Find out, and let us know."

"Well, I'll go up to John's to-morrow, and see Miss McCord."

He went up to the pine woods, and the next evening after tea returned. Helen and Mrs. Lawson had consulted. The plan of the overseer was a good one, and they would adopt it, and when he reported that the place, with a comfortable log house, with shed rooms and kitchen and other outhouses, with one hundred acres under fence and eight hundred in timber, with twenty-five head of cattle and fifty head of sheep, could be bought for $3,000 cash.

Helen had never had any business transactions with anybody. If she wanted money her father gave it to her, if she wanted dry goods she sent an order to Rogers & Ellis, and they were sent, and so with all she needed; but now she must arrange for a considerable sum of money and take new responsibilities. Nothing so develops people as necessity, and the necessity was here. So the carriage was ordered, and Helen went with Mr. Jones to the railroad, and thence to Savannah, where she saw Mr. Harris. He fully agreed with her about the propriety of the purchase, and as there was still a balance of the money borrowed to Capt. Lawson's credit, and as Helen's mother was authorized to use it, the pine woods plantation was bought, and the family had their summer home fixed there.

Mr. William Jones, the overseer, remained at the rice plantations the larger part of the time, night and day. In the summer he removed his family to his old place, near his brother's, so he was enabled to watch over both plantations.

Uncle Jack was the real supervisor of "Pine Grove" under Helen's direction. The sheep had been sheared, and the wool had been shipped, as usual, to the Roswell Woolen Mills to be made into kerseys; but Uncle Jack said: "Miss Helen, why for you no git some cards, so dese lazy niggers can card dey own wool for to make dey close, an' not send 'em so fur away?"

"Well, that is a good idea, Uncle Jack, and I'll send to Savannah for a box of wool cards, and some for cotton, too."

So the cards were sent for, and Mrs. Jones had a half-dozen looms put up, and the women taught how to spin and weave.

Mrs. Lawson found Helen a thoughtful helper at all times, and although the girl tenderly loved her father and brother and could not but feel their absence, she saw that the best way to show her love for them was not by complaining at their absence, but by caring for the things in which they were concerned.

At first there was no want of anything; but the thoughtful Helen saw that with the ports all closed, and with the unusual demand that the war made for manufactured articles, there must soon come scarcity, and so she began at once to provide against it. She agreed with her manager that to live at home and buy but little was the only true course, and that it was wise to get now such things as she might need hereafter. So she laid in full supplies of all the heavy groceries still in the markets.

She found time, in the midst of all her labors, to give the mail boy, who called every three days at "Pine Lodge" on his way to the railway from Riceboro, something for those away. When Roger was at Sewell he received this long letter from her:

"PINE LODGE," September 15, 1861.

My Dear Roger: We received your letter from Lynchburg just before you left, and also yours from Jackson's River. Since then we have heard nothing; and as you were at the jumping off place, we do not know but that you have jumped.

We were very sorry to hear of your attack of heart disease. I am afraid you don't really want to get the *Payne* out of your heart. I can't say so much for her. She has doubtless forgotten the young Georgia cracker by this time, and has taken a young officer under her pious care.

Well, we are here. What do you think of my going into the land market? Papa suggested to mamma to get a country home at Walthourville; but every house in the village was taken, and we had no time to build. We could not go up the country, and so mamma and I concluded to come here. We found that we could buy the place, but could not rent it, and as Mr. Jones thought it would be a good trade, and as Mr. Harris said that he could manage about the money, we bought it. We moved up over a month ago. We did not care to get away from "Lawson Place" till we were obliged to, and you know that it is not safe to remain there later than the 1st of August.

I have got to be a regular manager. Old Uncle Jack is my factotum. We bought all of Mrs. McCord's chickens, ducks, and geese, and I have become quite a poultry raiser. Then I have taken some lessons in weaving and spinning, not doing it myself, but learning how it ought to be done.

Poor mamma is doing her best to keep up and be cheerful as possible, and I feel like I must take all the care from her that I can.

You asked about company. Mr. Jones's daughter Nancy stays with us. She is very neat and good-natured, and is a pleasant companion. We are only half a mile from Serg. Jones, and his people, or some of them, are over here every day. We have the Methodist Church in a mile from us, and a Sunday school which I attend, and the Varnadoes live not very far off, and come over and spend a day with us now and then, and sometimes we go over there. Then we have the weekly Richmond and Savannah papers, and I am reading old books and old magazines. Write us every time you get a chance, and tell us everything.

Affectionately your sister, HELEN.

Roger's mother added to Helen's letter.

P. S.—Helen has written you a long letter, and I will just add a line. O my dear boy, what a precious girl she is! She knows how much I miss you, and she seems anxious to take all care from me and do all my thinking. She found no Sunday school here, but though she is so timid, she began one, and now she has at least forty little children, who meet her every Sunday. She leads the music, reads the Bible, directs the school, and with the help of the old class leader, Mr. Andrews, they say she manages the school splendidly. The people about here like her so much, and are so kind to us all. Be a good boy as you have always been. God keep you safely. Take good care of my dear Roger.

Your affectionate MOTHER.

CHAPTER IX.

GAINING EXPERIENCE.

*The King of France with forty thousand men
Marched up the hill and then marched down again.*

I SUPPOSE that if the authorities in Montgomery or Washington had known what would have resulted the "Star of the West" would never have tried to reach Fort Sumter; and if she had, the Confederate battery on the island would never have fired on the old flag; and I'm sure that if the Federal and Confederate authorities had been wise the campaign in Western Virginia would never have been undertaken, for a more useless and costly campaign on both sides was never conducted. The government at Richmond believed it of vital importance that West Virginia should be held. They did not know enough of its geography to know that it would hold itself. So when Gen. Lee, who saw the folly of any further advance toward the Ohio, or of any further effort to hold these wild hills against an invader who had no use for them, had gone back to Camp Alleghany, and thence to Richmond, the stout old Gen. Floyd was left alone. Who planned the campaign which

(93)

like to have ended at Cotton Hill in the capture of the brigade I never knew, but somebody had some ideas that did not materialize. The supplies that were needed for the army at Sewell had to be hauled sixty miles over wretched roads, and all the teams which had been taken from the farms were not sufficient to bring the food needed for the army. To march down the pike after Rosecrans was not wise, and so it was decided to move on his flank and get behind him. I suppose our general commanding expected somebody to move down the turnpike on the enemy's front while he crossed the Kanawha, and strike him in the rear—a very good plan if it could have been carried out. The army never knew where we were going, but we retraced our steps to Meadow Bluff and thence to New River and over it, or rather through it, we went into Raleigh, and then through Fayette County to Miller's Ferry and Cotton Hill, and from there Roger wrote to Helen:

Cotton Hill, Fayette County, Va., September 1, 1861.

Dear Helen: We are here at last. I thought we were out of the world when we got to Sewell, but now we are away on the other side. We struck our camp at Sewell and moved back to the Meadows, and then the army turned toward the New River. The pioneers had gone ahead to make the road passable, and we managed to get along, but it was with great difficulty. Such a wild country I never supposed was in Virginia. There was a squad of us youngsters who concluded to strike across the country by a neighborhood road from our New River camp. Just before night we came to the stock farm of an old Virginia gentlemen. Just to think of finding out here in these wild hills and meadows one of the most delightful and elegant families you ever saw. The girls are highly educated, and in the straggling house of a half-dozen single-story rooms was a fine piano, and the first music except that of the fife and bugle I have heard since we left Lynchburg we had the night I was there. And what a nice supper we had. I was sorry to leave them the next morning, but we had to go. Our camp was on the east side of New River, in a beautiful little valley, where there was a sulphur spring. They have the white sulphur, the blue sulphur, the red sulphur, the salt sulphur, the black sulphur, and this is the green sulphur. You know an army has much more to do than to march and fight. There are roads to make, provisions to haul, and the sick to provide for, and just now we have our share of sick folks you may be sure. Where have all these soldiers been raised, that they have never had the measles and mumps and other diseases which every well-bred boy ought to have before he is twelve years old? but right out here in the woods, where there are few doctors and no medicine, to be getting sick is too bad. Our chaplain and the surgeons have their hands full. We had to swim the river on our horses. In we went and over we went. Daisy swam beautifully. Then we were in the woods sure enough, and we are not out of them yet. We passed through two small villages and came out into a very nice settlement where there were some right neat homes, and before I knew where we were I found we were in a skirmish. The yankees were on the other side of the river, at the "Hawk's Nest," as it is called, and were picketing the river banks when our advance came in sight of them. There was a good deal of shooting at long range between their sharpshooters and ours. I fired my first gun, but I don't think I hit the yank, because I saw him run; and as I was lying behind a log, I don't think I was in much danger.

Well, we are living high, if to be high up in the air can be called so, but otherwise our fare is but middling. Jack is thoroughly "disencouraged," he says. "Dis here country, Mass Roger," he sadly remarked last night, "nebber was made for a decent man to lib in. De idee dat Capt. Roger Lawson should hab to eat de kin' of flour dey gib us, an' hab nothin' but black sorghum sirup; and I hab to make him biskuts with no lard, no soda, no buttermilk, no nothin'. I wish dem yanks would stay at home or leave here, and let us git back to Liberty."

Our flour is made by grinding wheat in a corn mill; and as it is not bolted, it is not pearly white. We are simply watching the yanks and waiting. It has been raining a great deal, and roads are bad; and as we are a hundred miles from our nearest railroad station, you may not wonder that we are somewhat anxious to know what is next. I hardly think old "Rosey" will try to cross the rivers (for we are in the bend where the New and Gauley make the Kanawha). The other day I went with papa and a party of explorers to the mouth of Loop Creek, on the Kanawha. This put us several miles behind the yankee camp. I think maybe Gen. Floyd thinks of crossing there, but I am a little afraid the Yank's may cross first and come up behind us. You never saw as wild a country as this. There are nothing but hills, hills covered with grass and apple trees, with now and then a tobacco field.

I will write you soon again. ROGER.

The camp was so located that the crossing of the New River by one detachment and the crossing of the Kanawha by another would completely cut off the whole brigade and capture it, for there was but one way of escape, southward down a narrow country road.

When Gen. Floyd found that neither Gen. Lee nor any one else came down the pike he saw that his campaign must be a failure and was now reluctantly getting ready to return to the railroad, to be nearer his supplies.

He had made his decision to do this none too soon, for the trap he had set for the Federals, they sprang on him. While Floyd was anxiously waiting for the move on Rosecrans, " Rosey" moved on Floyd. Two detachments of the Federal army crossed the river—one the New River, at Bowyer's Ferry; one the Kanawha, at Loop Creek—and each aimed to join their forces behind Floyd. They expected to bag the game easily, but the old general was too quick for them, and when they drew the mouth of the net together the birds had flown. Roger, however, wrote Helen a letter which tells the story better than I can:

CAMP MISERY, RALEIGH CO., VA., Nov., 1862.

My Dear Helen: If old " Rosey " had been a little quicker in his movements, I don't think you would have had a letter from this place, which, as you see, I call Camp Misery—why, you will see as I write on. I must claim, however, the credit for the name, and I don't think the old general would let me go without a court-martial if he found I called it so disrespectfully. You know I told you that I was afraid the yanks would cross below us, and so they did. Late one afternoon an orderly came for papa to come to headquarters. As I am acting as his orderly, I went with him. The old general sat there as quiet and as grim as ever. He said very calmly to papa, as if he did not know anything: " Colonel, you had best order in your pickets and have your wagons packed. I have decided to take a better position, nearer our base of supplies. See to it that all is done quietly and carefully." Just then a citizen came galloping up, and asked for the general. He seemed greatly excited. "The yankees are marching up the road from Loop Creek, two thousand strong," he said; "I saw them cross, and came in a gallop across the hills to let you know." The old general smiled, a quiet smile, and said very kindly and calmly: "All right, Squire; we are ready for them; they are doing just what I hoped they would do." Then while he was here another citizen came at full speed, and said: "General, them yanks has been a crossing all night at Bowyer's Ferry, and are marching this way." "That's all right, Mr. Hughes," said the general; "they will fall into the trap that I have set for them; don't you be alarmed." I don't know that the old general told the truth; and between you and me I don't think he did; but he looked very much like he was saying what he thought was so. Well, we did not wait long. The wagons were loaded, the pickets from down at the ferry came galloping in, and the infantry was put in marching condition. We were to keep in the rear. The tents could not be carried, and some of the least valuable stores were put in front of them to be burned. The tents were left standing and fires built in front of them, and our battalion was distributed among them, so that it would look as if the army was here still; and as soon as it was dark the army began its "advance backward," as Jack says. The wagons had gone ahead, and the artillery had taken its position near the only road, which came from the south, to the pocket in which we were.

After the infantry were off, we and Col. McCausland's battalion came up behind. We fully expected to have a brush with the yanks at the road; but we passed it and were safe out of the trap by midnight. One of them, whom we captured, said that Gen. Benham had halted his troops just a mile from this road we crossed. Had our boys known that the yanks were only a mile from where they were, and that we would all have been captured or cut to pieces if we had remained till morning, I think they would have grumbled less at this all-night march.

Early in the morning Col. Craghan, who had charge of the Kentucky Dragoons, rode by us down the Loop Creek road. In a little while we heard firing, and the Dragoons came galloping back without their leader, who was killed. They were followed by a troop of yankee cavalry; but our men opened fire on them with their carbines, and they were checked, and when the two guns of our artillery sent their shells whizzing down the road they fell back to their infantry. We fully expected a battle, and the army was in line; but strangely enough they did not advance, and we continued our retreat. The old general and his staff remained in the rear. The sick were in front; then came the wagon train, and then the infantry and light artillery, and the cavalry came last.

I had been all night in the saddle. So when the army halted as it did, and formed in line, as I wrote you, ready to give battle, we were ordered to dismount and fight on foot. Poor Daisy had no breakfast, and poor master had a piece of Graham hoecake for his. We remained here all day fasting, and late in the afternoon, when our pickets reported that Gen. Benham had gone back and there was no enemy in sight, our infantry began its march again. We came marching last, only followed by the pioneers, who blocked up the road by cutting down great trees across it. At last we were ordered into camp. The wagon train could go no farther, for it was as dark as Egypt. We were at the foot of an immense hill, and there was not level ground enough to spread a blanket. We went up the hill—Lieut. Bacon, Serg. Jones, papa, and I—and found a place to sleep. Jack came to our help, and we made a hasty shelter. It was made of small saplings and brush, over which we spread our oilcloths, and was so fixed that one fork held all up. I was so tired and worn-out and sleepy that I could hardly wait for Jack to broil some beef and make some coffee, and then I threw myself under this shelter on my blanket, and was soon asleep. It so happened that I was near the supporting fork, and in the night I dreamed that a tree was falling on us, and crying out, "A tree is falling! a tree is falling!" I caught hold of and jerked down the fork, and the whole thing fell. They all scrambled out from the bushes, and just then such a rain fell as you never saw; but we built a huge log fire, dried our clothes, and sat by it till morning.

Such roads! such roads! I saw a mudhole so deep that a man on a horse would have been swallowed up in it; but we pressed on, and just at dark we reached this camp. It is by the side of a wild mountain brook, and the mountains are on every side. We built large fires, cooked our rations, and laid down under what "flys" we had, and the next morning woke to find our blankets and tent flys covered with snow.

Some one is going to Dublin, on the railroad, to-day; and as I have a chance to send you this letter, I will wait no longer. How long we are going to stay here I cannot say, but I heard Gen. Wharton tell papa that it was likely that we would go back to the railroad at once, and that some of us would go to South Carolina and some to Kentucky. Tell mamma that we are all right, and that I have seen a great sight of things to tell her about. Tell old Jack that young Jack says if "Mass Roger ever gits back to Libbaty and brings him back, he never wants to see nothin' higher dan a Salamander hill agin." He says "he's seed mountings nuff to last him a lifetime."   ROGER.

The old general reluctantly gave up his cherished plan. He would gladly have wintered in this wild section, and have been ready to move down on the Kanawha Valley, resting only on the banks of the Ohio, but the tide was against him, and orders came from headquarters for Floyd's Brigade to report to Gen. Buckner at Fort Donelson, in Kentucky, and for Lawson's Battalion of Georgia cavalry to report to Gen. Drayton at Hardeeville, S. C. Before these orders came the men had been paid off and they were anxious to send their money to their families, and as they had great confidence in Roger they asked that his father would permit him to take this money to them. As Roger was not needed specially, and as Gen. Floyd had no objection to giving him a furlough, he was permitted to go to Georgia, and he started. His letter from Wytheville will tell of how narrow an escape he made from an unlooked-for danger:

WYTHEVILLE, November 15, 1861.

Dear Helen: I am here waiting for the train to take me to Georgia, and I will write you a line. The men of the battalion were paid their money at Camp Misery, and as there was no way to get it to their families but by hand, they asked papa if I might not take it for them. Papa hesitated, for bringing $5,000 so far among so many dangers is not a pleasant thing; but they told him they could trust me, and that their families needed the money and there was no other way to get it to them, and so papa went to see Gen. Floyd and he told him that if he thought it best he would give me a furlough, and so I got my furlough. There was $5,000 in Charleston bank bills. Serg. Jones had a money belt which he loaned me, and I packed the money in it and bade good-bye to Camp Misery, and started out on my journey a few hours before dark. I was alone, but I joined a Virginia cavalryman who knew the country, and we rode about sunset some two or three miles off of the road to get a place to stay all night. We found a good place, where I had the first square meal I've had in a long time. The old fellow had buckwheat cakes and rye coffee, sweetened with maple sugar—they call it tree sugar up here. He had some beef ribs stewed and the nicest butter and milk. He was as clever as he could be, and his old wife was as motherly as mamma. I slept gloriously, and after a good breakfast next morning I rode with my friend back to the main road. Here he parted from me, as he was going back to camp, and I rode on alone. It was a pretty dreary ride, the ground was frozen, the air was keen, and the heavy forests were covered with sleet and ice. I was pulling away when I heard some one coming as fast as the bad roads would permit, when who should it be but Serg. Jones? He had his carbine and two navy pistols. When he saw me he halloed at me; and when he came up he said: "Well, my boy, I never was as glad to see any one in my life. I was afraid that I would never see you any more."

"How now, Sergeant?" I said. "Did you think I'd run away with your money?"

"No; but last night Carson, from the Rifles, deserted and took his gun with him and followed your trail. Where have you been?"

"I went with Corporal Brent to old Squire Tuckweld's."

"Well, thank God! That may have saved your life. The Colonel sent me posthaste after you, and said that I was to go with you to Princeton. The General said that you must not go as you intended, by Pack's Ferry to Dublin, but go to Princeton, and thence to Wytheville. "Here, Jenkins," the Sergeant said to his attendant, "ride back to camp and tell them that Roger is all right."

We got to Princeton, a little village hidden away in the mountains, and at night found quarters not far from it, and then began our journey over the Alleghanies to Wytheville. I thought that I had been in the mountains before, but now, as I started to go across them, I found what it meant to be in the wild Alleghanies sure enough.

The Sergeant, who was to join the battalion at Dublin, was with me, so it was not so lonely as it would have been otherwise, and O the scenery was so grand! Ten thousand times ten thousand icicles hung from the green pines, and the sunbeams flashed from tree to tree, from mountain top to mountain top. We found comfortable quarters on the banks of Wolf Creek, at a farmer's home, and the next day about noon we came out into a cove in the mountain, and O what a lovely sight this little valley, with its beautiful brick house, was! We went to the gate, and they cheerfully took us in. The cove was called Crockett's Cove, and old Mr. Crockett lived in it. He has such a sweet wife, and O such charming daughters! You have no idea how good these Virginia farmers and their families are. They were just as kind to me as if I were their son, and although I was with them but a little while they seem as though they had known me all my life. You may know the Sergeant and I had a good time. We did not go on to Wytheville till the next day, and while I was waiting for the train the Sergeant, leading Daisy, went up toward Dublin, which is about forty miles from here. Here he expects to meet the battalion. I am coming home for a few days while the battalion is getting to its new field at Hardeeville, so you need not be surprised to see me at any time.   ROGER.

CHAPTER X.

A WEEK AT HOME.

ROGER was impatient to get home; but although he was not delayed on the railroad, he had a half-dozen places at which to stop, and a number of people to see before he could hope to reach Savannah; but he did his duty faithfully, and saw the money which had so nearly cost him his life safe in the hands of those to whom it was sent.

Carson was last seen in a mountain gorge on New River. He had evidently intended to meet his unsuspecting young comrade, and, deluding him with a plausible tale, when he had reached an obscure spot he designed to murder him, secure the money, and escape.

At last all the parcels except those intended for the members of the Liberty Troop had been disposed of, and Roger left Savannah on the Atlantic and Gulf road for Fleming. No one knew when he was coming, and no one came to meet him. As he left the train he met the good-natured old agent, Mr. Clark, and inquired about a conveyance.

"Well, Capt. Roger," he said, "there hain't

a sign of a critter on my place 'ceptin' old Beck. She is about thirty-five year old and is mighty true, but she's powerful slow. She'll take you thar if you give her time, but I tell you now she ain't a gwine to be pushed, but she is a heap better than walkin', and I'll have her brought out."

Beck was a well-kept and very unpretending mule. Her long ears hung listlessly down, and her head was bent very humbly to the earth. Roger mounted, and Beck moved as she did in the plow, and had done for a score of years, with steady step and slow. Roger urged her forward with earnest words, but she heeded not. He struck her with the switch which he had in his hand, but it made no impression on her sensibilities; and at last, when all else had failed, the eager boy struck his sharp spur in old Beck's side. She winced, then stopped, and turned her head back with a look of blank amazement, and then moved forward, but she never changed her gait. "Well, old lady," said Roger, "you must go as you please, so as I can't get you to go my gait I'll go yours." It was a weary ride, but it ended at last. It was nightfall when old Beck stopped at the gate. Leaping from her back, the boy rushed into the house and threw himself into his mother's arms. She did not know when he was coming, but she looked for him every hour, and was watching for him when he came. Helen was next, and then the negroes all crowded around him. He had been gone but a few months, but it seemed to those who loved him that it had been years. His mother's pale face told what she had been suffering, and Helen was transformed into a real matron. Old Uncle Jack, of course, came to ask after young Jack, his hopeful son. "Yes, Uncle Jack, said Roger, "Jack has become quite a soldier. He likes soldiering, all but the marching and the fighting. He was in camp one day and a yankee battery began to shell us, and when the shell came whistling into the camp I looked for Jack, but he was gone. He came back after the gun quit firing, and I asked where he had been. 'Lor', Mars Roger,' he said, ' dat ting come right at me. It nebber tried to ketch nobody but me, and when I seed it a coming I heard it say, " Run, nigger, run!" and I runned, I did. I ain't afeard of no yankees, but I cain't bar to have a whole cannon just shootin' at me. I tell you I cain't.' He told me to give you a heap of howdy, and say that if he can get a furlough he will come home Christmas."

Roger sat by his mother's side, with her hand in his, like a lover. He would stroke her hair and kiss her fair brow as he did when a child. That was one reason I loved the boy. He knew his mother's worth, and loved her so tenderly.

John Jones, the oldest son of the Sergeant, stayed at " Pine Lodge " at night, and took a kind of oversight of the place, giving Helen such help in directing things as she needed. As for managing the hands, Uncle Jack did that better than any other one could; the only trouble with him was that he was too hard on them.

John was a devoted Methodist. He had been raised in a family where they had prayer night and morning, and when he came to spend the night at Mr. Lawson's he was not reluctant to keep up there the custom he had always followed at home. So they had family worship, which he conducted. The negroes came in; the Bible was read; the hymn was carefully lined and earnestly sung; and John prayed, if not learnedly, yet fervently. After he had prayed God to take care of the father and the son in the army, and now when the boy was at home again, his voice faltered as he thanked God for his safe return. He prayed very earnestly that as Roger's life had been spared it should be devoted to God's service.

Roger went over the next day to see the Sergeant's family, and to carry them the money that the Sergeant had sent to them, as well as the letter that he had written. The days went too rapidly by. He saw the families of the troopers, and gave them the tidings from their loved ones.

On Sunday at old Taylor's Creek meetinghouse Dr. Farmer was to preach the funeral of a young Stovall, who was killed at the first battle of Manassas. The Doctor was once a traveling preacher, then he located and studied medicine, and for many years he had been a physician and a planter. George Stovall he had known from his childhood. He had baptized him, he had received him into the Church, and when his body was brought home he had read the funeral service over his grave. In those days the funeral sermon was often preached months after the subject was dead. There was a great crowd of people, and a great many of them were young people. The Doctor took advantage of the occasion to preach a very earnest sermon to young people. He showed them that religion was suited to them; that its very restraints were the sources of truest happiness; that there was no time in life in which religion could be more enjoyed than in youth, and at no time was piety more practicable. He warned them against the danger of delay. He spoke of young Stovall as one who had never given his father's heart a single pang, of how beautifully he lived, and of how grandly he died.

There was much feeling among his hearers. Many came and gave him their hand, in token of a determination to take Jesus as their Saviour, and, to his mother's great joy, among them was Roger. The "Church door" (as the Methodists call the opportunity for candidates to present themselves for union with the Church) was opened, and Roger went forward.

His Presbyterian mother looked on with a blank amazement, and yet her face was lit with joy. When they came home, she said: "Well, my son, I am so glad that you joined the Church. I have often prayed God to make you a Christian, but I never prayed him to make you a Methodist." Perhaps Mrs. Lawson remembered that this was somewhat the same thing Mr. Spurgeon's mother told him.

It had been no sudden impulse, for Roger had intended to unite with the Church and give his life to God's service for some time, and he was not willing to wait. He knew that the certificate of the Methodist Church would take him into the Presbyterian, which he thought it likely he would join when he went back to Medway.

CHAPTER XI.

CAMPAIGNING ON THE COAST.

ROGER had been at home only a few days when a letter from his father written from Dublin, Va., brought the news that the battalion was to report to Gen. Drayton at Hardeeville, S. C. He wrote Roger to join it there in about ten days.

The days sped with rapid pace, and were soon gone. Roger went by railway, and found the battalion in a temporary camp on the sand hills beyond the Savannah River, where the little village of Hardeeville was located. They were, however, to remain here only a few days, and were to camp at Bluffton, fifteen miles below on the seacoast.

The part of South Carolina where their camp was located was the oldest portion of the State. Near the camp was May River, on which the first settlements in the State had been made by the French three hundred years before, and here the English settlers had established themselves permanently two hundred years before.

The islands on the coast had been famous for producing the most beautiful long staple cotton, and the rice plantations on the main were on all the rivers where the water was fresh. There had been a very large number of negroes on the plantations. For generations these people on the coast and the sea islands had lived in great luxury. The sea gave them the best fish and finest oysters. The marsh grass and the wire grass of the pine woods furnished them pasturage for their cattle, and the rice and corn produced on every plantation furnished them breadstuff. When the Federal navy swept down on Port Royal and captured it, the people along this coast were seized with a panic, and gathering up their slaves, and leaving behind all their property which could not be moved, they fled to the interior of Georgia and South Carolina. They had their residences in a few pleasant settlements, where they could have the advantage of churches and schools and health. Among the little hamlets which served for a summer home was Bluffton, immediately on May River. It was a beautiful little village among the live oaks and pines. The steamers came triweekly to the wharf on their way from Charleston to Savannah, and thus brought the planters into close contact with the outer world. The little Episcopal and Methodist Churches furnished the inhabitants with religious services. Here, in an easy, quiet, inoffensive way the planters lived; but when Port Royal fell they abandoned everything, and fled, and when Roger came to the camp he found the soldiers in beautiful homes, some furnished still with good furniture, which had been deserted by their panic-stricken owners. Libraries of books, mahogany chairs, bureaus, and sofas were left for the accommodation of the troops. The Colonel quartered them in the vacated houses, and they began a season of camping out which was specially delightful.

Roger had now taken his part in all the hard work of the common trooper. How he engaged his time, and some of his adventures, he can best tell himself:

BLUFFTON, S. C., December, 1861.

Dear Helen: If our camp in West Virginia was Camp Misery, this ought to be called Camp Paradise. You have no idea of the change. The rich people that used to live here took fright when Beaufort and Port Royal fell, and fled to the upcountry. They left nearly everything behind them, and now, instead of being out in the cold on the mountains unsheltered, behold me in a lady's boudoir. The mahogany bureau stands as she left it. The bedstead and washstand are both here. The village was a deserted village sure enough, not a living being left in it when we came. Since then some few have come back, but not to stay.

Bluffton is what its name would lead you to suppose it was. It is a bluff on the river, with a wide stretch of pine lands back of it. How beautiful the river is here, and how beautiful and how charming are the islands which dot it, I cannot tell you. We are here to picket the coast, and see that the yanks don't cross over and cut the railroad between Savannah and Charleston. Bluffton is a good place to picket from. We lead the most luxurious lives. Lieut. Bacon has his dog and shotgun with him, and as he rides around to see after the posts he carries his gun, and brings back partridges every day. Serg. Jones is a good fisherman, and such sheephead and trout as we do have! We have to drill every day—that is, those who are not on picket duty—but when the drill is over we have nothing to do, so we get out the boats and go rowing and fishing. Such fun we do have! The kinds of fish that I have seen and caught I could hardly count. The sting ray is an awful fellow, with his diabolical look and long tail and awful barb, which he wears just coming out of his back. This barb he sends into his victim, and it holds him like a fishhook. The other day I caught a shark two feet long, and carelessly put my fingers into his mouth to pull out my hook, and he *caught me!* I was caught for sure; but the Sergeant came to my rescue, and prized the shark's jaws open. He had bitten through my finger nail.

I have had to take my time standing picket. There are four of us on each post; but it is awfully lonesome to stand on the river shore, and watch for two hours before you are relieved. We are looking for the gunboats every day, but they do not come.

You remember when we were at Catherine's Island to have seen a school of porpoises. You know what a noise they make in the water. As they come rolling over and over, and splashing the water, they make a sound like a boat in motion. Some of our boys are from the mountains, and never saw a gunboat or a "porpus," as Jack calls them. They were on picket on the bluff. The moon was half full, and they could dimly see from where they stood the river winding around the bend.

They heard at midnight a sound they had never heard the like of before, and they saw the waters in motion. They did not stand on the order of their leaving. Firing their carbines at the supposed enemy, they mounted their horses, and dashed back to camp. The bugler sounded "Saddles," and we were in short order dashing down the road to the bluff. There were neither yanks nor gunboats, but the sea pigs were having a big time in the river.

We are having a jolly time, with enough work to do to keep us out of mischief. Our chaplain comes to the camp every week and spends a few days with us. He has preaching and prayer meeting in the Methodist church, and we enjoy the services very much.

Tell mamma that we got the box of good things, and we have royal dinners, and Jack is in his glory. Love to everybody. Tell Mrs. Jones that the Sergeant messes with us, and that he is getting to be real fat.

Affectionately, ROGER.

Campaigning on the coast was a monotonous business. The videttes went to the posts in the evening and morning, and rode back again. The troops received the daily papers from Charleston and Savannah, and their mail every day. Some of them had their wives to come to the camp to see them. The Federals exchanged half-playful shots across the waters of the small bays with the videttes on the other side, but the bullets fell harmlessly in the water. Roger was so much better acquainted with the state of things, however, that I will let him tell his story:

MAY RIVER, May, 1861.

My Dear Helen: We have moved our camp. If you will get the map of South Carolina, and look to its lowest point below Savannah, you will see the point where we are. The place is called Box's. The old farmhouse, which is a hundred years old, has been vacated, and we have some of our troops housed in it. It is most beautifully located in a grove of oaks, and is surrounded on every side by salt water. At certain times of the tide we are on an island. Our videttes are distributed from this point to all the country around. There is not a soul near us except some old negroes on the Drayton and Pope places. These old places interest me very much. They are so old that I cannot but bring up the pictures of the wonderful changes which have passed over this section since they were settled; and yet, while the houses are old and the fields are old, and the negroes who were born here are old, there is very much of the country which is as wild as when the Indians were here. A few old men hang about their homes, but the larger part of the inhabitants are gone to the interior. There is not a lady nearer than Hardeeville, which is twenty miles away. There used to be some here evidently, for some dainty-looking shoes, which were once on a woman's foot, but were worn out long ago, are lying around. One of our boys got one the other day and made some tracks in the sand, and looked fondly at them.

You know that Fort Pulaski has fallen. One of our posts is in full view of it, and by climbing upon the lower limbs of a live oak I had a good sight of the bombardment. I could see a long trail of smoke from the batteries of Gilmore as the shells moved on the effective work. I could see the smoke of our guns as they replied, and could hear the report across the water. All day long the guns were sounding. I did not think that the fort would fall; but the next day we could see that her guns were still, and then we had the news of her surrender. But I have written you a long letter. Love to everybody.

Yours, ROGER.

The winter climate in this part of South Carolina is really ravishing, and even the spring and early summer are quite pleasant. There were quite a number of refugees at the village where the railway station was, and the fair maidens used to visit the camp occasionally, much to Roger's enjoyment. Sometimes they dined with the officers, and sometimes they made an evening party and brightened the camp with their merriment. Thus the summer wore away. The chaplain had good books which he gave the men, and there was prayer meeting and preaching every Sunday. Then there was the daily drill, and the picketing, and the constant care of the horses. The mail came every day, and finally Roger's enjoyment reached its height when his mother and Helen came to spend a month in the camp. The enemy made no movement. The battles were joined around Richmond, and the seven days' fight was over, and the order came for Drayton's Brigade to report at Richmond to Gen. Lee, and await orders; and the most delightful episode of the war, to Roger, ended. Henceforth there was no holiday soldiering; it was stern work, and much of it.

CHAPTER XII.

INFANTRY SERVICE IN NORTHERN VIRGINIA.

THE battalion of troops which was commanded by Col. Lawson was cavalry, but it was connected with a battalion of infantry and a company of artillery, and formed a legion. When the troops were ordered to Virginia it was decided that the infantry should be raised to a regiment and the legion dissolved, and Col. Lawson, who was second in command, was given the regiment, while the colonel was given a brigade. Roger was transferred from the troop and made a sergeant major. It was to report at Richmond and await orders. The colonel of the regiment was entitled to forage for two horses, and so Daisy was taken along.

The troops were packed in freight cars and transported to Richmond. There was little to interest in the wearisome travel to Richmond, but at last the city was reached, and the regiment marched six miles down the river to Chaffin's Bluff, where it went into camp. There was little to do in camp, so Roger was permitted to go to the city every day. Richmond, whose fame is world-wide since it was the capital of the short-lived Confederacy, is an interesting place to visit, and Roger wrote Helen how it appeared to him in those late days of the summer of 1862:

CHAFFIN'S BLUFF (near Richmond), August, 1862.

Dear Helen: We are here now in camp. Our camp is six miles below Richmond, on a high bluff on the James River. Drewry's Bluff is just on the other side of the river, and batteries with heavy guns are planted in front of us. I think we are only here for a short time, and will soon be ordered to the front. You know I am no longer an orderly, but the sergeant major of my regiment. The infantry I do not like quite as well as I do the cavalry, but we are not so continuously in motion, and as papa has two horses I have the full use of my pretty Daisy, and when my duties do not keep me in camp I take advantage of my privileges. I go to Richmond nearly every day. The ride along the James is an interesting one; some of the farmhouses, or country seats rather, are very handsome. We pass through a rather rough section of the city called "Rocketts," and then through what was evidently the old city, until we reach the capitol and the more aristocratic part of it. I was struck by nothing in Richmond so forcibly as by the beautiful statue of Washington, with the statues of the great men around the base.

The city is full of soldiers. Brigadiers are so common that nobody notices their stars, and captains and lieutenants are nobodies, and as for a poor sergeant major he is out of sight. I saw the President the other morning at St. Paul's Church with his wife and his little son and daughter. He is a very gentlemanly, quiet-looking man who is a great deal less assuming than Corporal Sykes was when he got his new uniform. Mr.

Benjamin, the Secretary of War, with his spectacles on his nose, is the very picture of Mr. Moses Cohen, whose store you visit in Savannah. I went in last Sunday night to hear Dr. Duncan, the famous Methodist preacher. Mr. Davis goes there every Sunday night. Dr. Duncan is a stout, young, smooth-shaved, dignified-looking preacher, and his style is very easy and graceful. He is very popular, and his church is always crowded. I do not find our camp life a bad one, though we have right hard fare now. There is nothing but hard-tack and beef. The coffee has given out, and we have to put up with any substitute we can get. Sometimes we can get supplies from Richmond, but there are so many people there that we find it difficult and very expensive to get anything good to eat. We are very unsettled, and I expect my next letter will be from some place nearer the front.

I begin now to see what war is. The hospitals are filled with sick and wounded men. The country around here is stripped of everything which makes a country agreeable, and there is nothing talked of now but news from the front.

Affectionately, ROGER.

A few days after this letter was written Col. Lawson was ordered by Gen. Drayton to report to the quartermaster in Richmond, who would furnish transportation to Gordonsville. The horses were to be ridden through the country, and Roger was granted leave of absence from the regiment and permitted to make the three days' journey through the country on horseback. He wrote Helen when he reached Gordonsville:

GORDONSVILLE, August, 1862.

Dear Helen: I arrived here yesterday, after a most interesting ride from Richmond to this place, where we are now in camp. The country around Richmond, after you leave the James River, is by no means fertile. I do not think it ever was. We went through Hanover County, and found ourselves, before night, in what are known as the "Slashes." Papa says Mr. Clay was born here, and was called the "mill boy of the slashes." The country is very flat and swampy, and the homes are old, and the farms worn out; and when I know that Patrick Henry and Henry Clay were both born here I don't think it takes good land to make good orators. We reached a nice, plain farmhouse in Louisa County by nighttime, and had good quarters. The next day we rode through a poor country, like that we had ridden through, till near noon, when we came into the most beautiful section and saw some of the most elegant farms I ever saw. We rode up to a handsome brick house, and asked for dinner. We were warmly received, and found ourselves in a most elegant and refined home. Dr. Pendleton was the name of our host, and he was a delightful host you may be sure. We had a grand dinner. It really looked as if we were expected guests and elaborate preparations had been made for us. We found good places to stop everywhere, and came, after three days of steady riding, to our regiment, which is camped in an old field here. There are quite a number of troops here, and they are evidently expected to go somewhere, but where I cannot conjecture. I hope you are all having a good time at "Pine Lodge." I am so glad mamma has such a daughter as you are. If the good Lord brings us safe home again, we will try to show you how grateful we are. Love to everybody.

ROGER.

The army was ordered to move very soon after Roger reached it. There was only time for rest, and to bring up the convalescent, when the order came to cook three days' rations and be ready to move at a moment's warning. The seven days' fight had been over for near two months, and the Confederates, though much weakened by their losses, were now recruited and ready for another campaign. The Federals were now trying to reach Richmond by Fredericksburg, and were on the east side of the Rappahannock. Jackson had been moving on the enemy in the Valley, and had cleared it of his opponents, and now it was evident that the Confederate army was changing front so as to meet Burnside on the banks of the Rappahannock. The army is always in profound ignorance of what is designed, and at night, the day after Roger reached Gordonsville, it was put in motion to go it knew not where. Roger wrote Helen of this all-night march as soon as the army made a little halt, which it did near a small place called Stevensburg, where the army stopped for a day or two:

STEVENSBURG, VA., August 5, 1862.

My Dear Helen: We have had a long march and have just gone into camp here, not far from the Rappahannock, and while we are resting I will write you a line.

We began our march from Gordonsville in the afternoon, and marched through as poor a country as you ever saw. The march was all night long, and just at sunrise we reached the Rapidan River. There was no bridge, so I wondered how the soldiers were going to cross the river when they reached it. I saw them plunge in, clothes and all, and come out dripping on the other side. They continued the march, wet as they were, and just as we reached the road which came down the other side of the river Gen. Jackson came marching by to take position on the heights below us. We were now in the forks of the Rapidan and Rappahannock, and went into camp about ten o'clock in the day.

We were thoroughly tired, and rested all day, waiting for Burnside to cross the river and attack us.

The next morning I went out sauntering near the camp, and seeing a poor-looking house by the wayside, I went in. The family in it were the fussiest people I ever saw. The old man was fussy, his wife was fussy, and his daughters were fussy, and they were at their best that morning. Some soldier had stolen the old man's horse, and the lamentation was loud and long over the loss of his last "critter," as he called it. I told him he had better go at once to the general, the man who had the three stars on his collar, and tell him about it. He had just gone in hot haste, when one of the girls of the family came up and said: "O mam, they have hung a man down thar by the spring." Sure enough, there was a poor fellow, in a new Confederate uniform, hanging by the neck dead. He was a spy, and had been caught with evidence that he was not only a spy, but that he had murdered an orderly, and the general sentenced him to be hung at once.

The Federals were just on the other side of the river, and we expected them to cross over and attack us every hour; but they went back to Fredericksburg, and are trying to reach Richmond again by way of Alexandria and Manassas. When Gen. Lee found that they were making that move he ordered us to march. We are here merely to rest a little while, and then I think we will move on toward Manassas.

LATER.—Last night the order came for the men to be ready

to move at daylight, and at daylight the whole brigade was in column in the road and marched on toward the river. We filed out into a grove of large trees and formed a line of battle. The skirmishers were sent to the river bank, and directly we heard the rattle of their rifles, and then our cannon opened and the Federal battery replied. The firing was brisk, and the shells swept through the woods, over our heads, and tore down great branches from the trees, and now and then cut a trunk in two and fell in our midst.

I tell you, Helen, there was no fun in lying there and taking a shelling. Now and then we heard a groan, and knew that some one was wounded. Our chaplain was called to see one of our soldiers whose leg had been torn off by a shell. The poor fellow said he was "going to heaven," and asked the chaplain to pray for him, and he knelt there where the shells were flying and asked God to bless the dying man.

We expected every moment for the yankee infantry to be on us; but they made no move, and after an artillery duel of about two hours the firing ceased and we went back to camp and rested the remainder of the day.

At this camp I made my first effort at cooking for myself, and succeeded only tolerably. I made a dough of the flour by mixing it with water in an old tin pan which belonged to one of the soldiers, and, as I had no frying pan nor oven, I dug a pit like a barbecue pit and laid some green sticks across that, and my dough on the frame, and then stuck my bacon on a hickory stick and held it to the fire. As the grease oozed out I held it over the bread, and so accomplished several ends.

I don't like war. I don't want to hurt the yanks, and I don't want them to hurt me. I am sorry for the poor people along the march whose fences are burned and whose stock is all killed. Our own army does almost as much harm to those on the line of march as the enemy's. War is more wasteful and fearful than you can conceive of; but we are in it, and we must get out.   ROGER.

P. S.—*Dear Mamma:* Don't be uneasy. God has taken good care of papa and me, and I hope we will both get back. Pray for us.

Your loving   ROGER.

The little artillery duel was merely a feint. Gen. Pope was massing his troops for a decisive battle at Manassas, and Gen. Lee was getting ready to meet him. The armies zigzagged through Culpeper, Prince William, and Fauquier, until at last they reached Bull Run again, where the second battle of Manassas was fought.

It is not my purpose to write a history of the war, nor even of the campaigns in which Roger had a part, but merely to give a young fellow's adventures as he tells them himself. If my young readers want an authentic history of this campaign, they must search many books of war records to find it; and then if they find it as it really was, they will be more fortunate than I have ever been. I am sure the best intentions of an historian are not certain to lead him to a correct account of events when the relation of them comes from so many' people who had different points of view, but I am sure Roger's story is just as correct as it claims to be. He wrote to "Pine Lodge" every opportunity, but he had no time for writing from the time he left

Stevensburg till Monday, after the second battle of Manassas, and then he wrote to Helen and his mother:

MANASSAS, August, 1862.

Dear Helen: I have not written you for near two weeks. We have been incessantly on the march, and I can only snatch the time while we are bivouacking here to try and catch up. I wrote you last from near a little village called Stevensburg. The next day after I wrote we were ordered to march. You know a soldier goes by faith. He has to obey. He never knows where he is going. He does not even see his commander. The adjutant of the regiment gives me my orders, and I give them to the captains, and they give them to the orderlies, and we do what we're told to do, and that's the end of it.

Marching on foot and riding are very different things, and while I might ride now and then, I prefer to share with the men, and so I tramp along as they do. Poor fellows, many of them are barefooted, and it hurts me to see that they sometimes leave bloody prints on the ground as they walk; but they are the merriest crowd you ever saw. They have names for the soldiers from each of the different States. The Georgia troops are called "Goober Grabbers;" the North Carolina, "Tar Heels;" the South Carolina, "Sand Lappers;" the Arkansas, "Travelers;" the Florida, "Crackers," etc. If they see a fellow with a new hat, they yell at him: "Come out of that hat." They make fun of everything but religion. I never saw one, however bad he was, who would not treat his chaplain respectfully. They will divide all they have with you, but I am sorry to say they are not remarkable for their honesty. One fellow stole my oilcloth the other day, and while our chaplain was praying with his eyes shut one of the reprobates stole his blanket.

We trudge along sometimes very slowly behind our wagon

trains, and of all wearisome things it is to march behind a hundred loaded wagons. Sometimes we take short cuts across the fields. The other day we were moving along across a field in which there was a small clump of woods. The Eleventh South Carolina had just reached the woods, when I saw the first company break in wild confusion, and with a yell they made haste and delayed not. They ran a little way, and then some of them fell down and rolled over in the grass. The second company followed suit, and so did the third. "Hornets! hornets!" yelled the crowd, and our regiment made a detour rapidly and gave the spiteful fellows abundant room.

You must know this constant tramping grows wearisome, especially when you don't know where you are going. Some parts of the country are very fertile, but the country generally is quite worn. We began to get near the mountains, and reached the railroad at a gap called Thoroughfare. Here I saw Gen. Lee for the first time during this campaign. You know I saw him first last year at Sewell Mountain, and then afterwards in South Carolina; but he has changed very much in looks since he has turned out his beard, and has a much older look and seems to be a stouter man than he was. He was very kind and courteous to every one, acknowledging my salute with a pleasant smile.

We were placed in a railroad cut at Thoroughfare Gap, and had to take another shelling. The enemy's battery, however, could not reach us, and their shells exploded on the hills beyond us. The only disaster to me was a piece of spent shell which fell right on my heart and which I picked up and put in my pocket. I gave it to a lady who lived in a farmhouse near by, and who kindly had given me my supper. Papa bears up very bravely and cheerfully. He is a great favorite with his men, and is especially kind to them.

There was a right sharp little skirmish near the Gap, but it did not amount to a great deal. The yanks soon saw that they could not get through the Gap, and they drew off toward Grovetown.

I do not think in all our marching we have ever had such a day as the day we left Thoroughfare. It looked as if man and beast would perish for water. There were no brooks, no rivers, no springs, and the wells were drawn dry; but about four o'clock in the afternoon we came to a spring, if such it might be called, in an old field. We had not been out of hearing of cannons for two weeks, and were used to it, and the fact that the yankee artillery was blazing away at us did not at all disturb us. We were, however, arranged on the field by companies, and were preparing to fill our empty canteens when we heard the shriek of a shell as it fell right in our midst and exploded, leaving two men dead and two wounded. We soon saw that we were in range of a masked battery, and leaving our wounded men to the care of the surgeons and chaplain and ambulance corps, we left there in quick time. Recklessness and courage are, the soldiers say, different things, and the man who would foolishly expose himself, or the general who would foolishly expose his brigade, are at as great a discount as cowards. We were sorry to leave our poor wounded men, but we were almost in rifle shot of the enemy.

All that afternoon we could hear the yells of Jackson's men on our left and the huzzas of the yanks. Who was the victor? This was the question. At last the dark came, and with it the news that old Jack was on top still. We lay on our arms all night, forbidden to speak above a whisper, and with the dawning the guns opened again. We were in Longstreet's Corps, and were on the extreme right wing. We lay in an old field, just out of range of the shells; and while we could not see, we could hear the roar of the guns, the yells and huzzas of the soldiers, and see the white smoke of the cannon. I climbed up on top of an old house near our regiment, and with papa's glass I had a good view of the fight. Gen. Lee and his staff were on a high hill to our left, where they could see the entire field. Away off to the left was Jackson's Corps. It was a long way from us, but I could see where it was posted, in a cut of the railroad just deep enough to give good protection. When I looked the battle was getting pretty hot, and I could see the line of Federals coming out of the wood and moving on Jackson. Then the smoke from the rifles and the smoke from the cannon covered the field. When it blew away I saw that the blue line was broken and was retreating; but those brave yanks came again and again, and then our infantry seemed to me to cease firing, and the Federals swept on the works apparently unresisted. But just then two battalions of artillery came dashing at a full gallop up to the railway cut behind the silent infantry, and before I could tell you they had unlimbered, and the guns poured out volleys of shot and shell. I saw Gen. Longstreet just before this dash away from Gen. Lee at a full gallop, and at the head of an Alabama brigade, followed by the division, he dashed on the center of the Federals, and their left and center both gave way. I then saw the aid come galloping toward us and the long roll sounded.

I was on the ground in a moment and at my place, and we were double-quicked to the field of battle; but when we were almost on the field the order came to "Halt! right about face, forward double-quick," and *we came back to the field we left.* Somebody blundered. Gen. Drayton heard that the enemy were enfilading us and brought us back to find the enemy, and *lo! they were a company of our own troops.* We could not now move rapidly, for we were completely done up, so we quietly marched back to the field again and moved steadily, but not on a run, up the hill to the extreme left of the Federals. The general of the division rode by us and told us to give the soldiers in front a cheer, and we did.

To hear the whistle of the balls as they swept by you was not as fearful as the shriek of the shells, but more dangerous. As papa rode into the fields poor Whitey got a ball through the neck and fell, but with his sword in hand his rider pushed forward on foot.

It was to me strangely dark. I could not think it was nightfall, but it was, and just as we entered the wood from which we were to move on the battery which we were to silence it became so dark that we could not see, and then came the command to halt. We were so nigh the yanks that we could hear them talk, but we could not see ahead of us. The general thought if we attempted an advance we would fire into each other, and so we came out of the battle without firing a gun.

Several of our men were wounded, but none were killed. Poor old Whitey is right badly hurt, but he may get well. Papa telegraphed mamma, to Fleming, and telegraphed Mr. Clark to send you the telegram. I will write again as soon as I get a moment to spare, but I must write to mamma now.

ROGER.

Roger to his mother:

MANASSAS, August, 1862.

My Dear Mamma: My letter to Helen will tell you all about our doings for the last two weeks, and I only write to you to tell you how much I love you, and how glad I am that God took such care of papa in the battle day before yesterday. I did not relish the battle; but I was not so much afraid for myself as for him, and when I saw poor Whitey reel as the bullet struck him I was scared almost to death; but papa leaped from his back, and with his sword waving he urged the boys on as if nothing had occurred.

I am so glad that you taught me to pray. If it had not been for that, I am afraid that I should not have escaped the dangers of camp life, and all the day of the great battle I found my heart

9

rising to God in prayer. I am so glad that we won the victory; but as I went over the field yesterday, I was so sorry for the suffering of our own folks and of the poor yanks that I could not rejoice in the victory won. The Federals sent a flag of truce, and Gen. Lee gave them full permission to go over the field and gather up the wounded. I did what I could. With some of the other boys, we searched for those who were most in need of help, and filled their canteens with water, and fixed them as comfortably as we could, and tried to cheer them. Our own wounded were gathered into the farmhouses all about, and many of them put in ambulances and sent to Warrenton.

I hate war. I expect to be a true soldier, and to fight as well as I can; but I hate war.

The good Lord bless you all! Papa cannot write; he is too busy, for he is now in command of the brigade. He tells me to write, and sends a heartful of love.   ROGER.

CHAPTER XIII.

THINGS IN LIBERTY.

WHILE Roger and his father were at the front Mrs. Lawson and Helen were having no easy time at "Pine Lodge." The earnest efforts of Mr. William Jones, the overseer, who was past the age of conscription, had not relieved them entirely from anxiety. The chief care was the father and son, and then how to provide for all their slaves and of all their interest was indeed a trying question. The coast was so exposed that it was certain that the negroes would be forced away from the plantation, if they did not wish to leave, and it was as certain that many of them would run away to the yankees as soon as they could get a chance. The cattle and stock, with all the horses and mules, would fall a prey to the marauders who could land on the coast.

So it was decided to move all that could be moved up to "Pine Lodge," and abandon for the time being the two plantations on Medway. There were houses to build, fields to open, and immediate needs to be supplied. There was a full crop of rice made in 1861, and the large crop of potatoes and corn which Mr. Jones had made at "Pine Lodge;" but it was necessary to live very closely. It was a struggle for subsistence. There was no money but Confederate money, and its purchasing power was not great.

Capt. Lawson had an investment in the stock of the Rosevelt Cotton Factory, and received dividends in cotton thread and in cloth; and this, with the busy hands of the spinners and weavers, supplied the negroes with clothes. Sugar cane, peanuts, upland rice, potatoes, and peas were planted, and while the negroes missed their patches and had to submit to privations which were not at all agreeable to them, and while some of them ran away from the farm, the most of them remained, and very faithfully aided their mistress in her exertions.

Helen's letters to Roger will tell of how grandly the brave girl bore herself under it all:

"Pine Lodge," August, 1862.

My Dear Roger: Yours from Stevensburg just received. Verily you are having a time. I hardly know where to catch you; but it may be that this will reach you, as it is sent by one of the Troop who has been at home on a furlough.

Well, we are doing very well. After the fall of Fort Pulaski last April, we saw that our removal from the coast could not be long delayed, and so Mr. Jones sent up twenty of the men, and they went to work to build the cabins. Happily father had bought a small sawmill outfit, and Mr. Jones had it moved up here. We needed to clear a great deal of land to put at once in peas for the people, and so we cleared the land and got timber for the mill at the same time. We soon had the cabins ready, and while there was a rest time we began to move everything but the growing rice to this place. We are now all pretty well moved, and until harvest we will be easy. We expect to send down a set of hands then to get in the rice; but their families will remain here.

We are quite comfortable. I am wearing my old clothes. I made my first hat out of palmetto the other day. We make our sugar, as you know, and we get from the Rosevelt Mill a few bales of cotton yarn every month, which not only supplies our wants, but which we can trade for bacon and other supplies. We have about used up our coffee, except a little that we keep for the preacher and for sick folks; but we get along pretty well on potato coffee and ground pea chocolate.

Don't you be worried about us. I have a beautiful suit of gray jeans just out of the loom for papa, and one for you, and you ought to see me in my brand new homespun. If you men will do your duty at the front, we will do ours at home.

I still keep up my Sunday school, and enjoy my work very much. I believe God will take care of you both, and I am trying to do what I know he wills for me to do at home. Mamma keeps as well as could be expected, but this constant anxiety presses her much.

God bless you, my dear, brave brother! I love you more than I can tell. Love to dear papa. HELEN.

CHAPTER XIV.

MARYLAND! MY MARYLAND!

THE stunning defeat of the Federal army only seemed to inspire the determined North with a sterner resolution to conquer at all costs, and slowly and stubbornly the Army of the Potomac fell back to Washington. I doubt if the capture of Washington was ever seriously contemplated by the Confederates. The fact was, the South knew she could not conquer the North; she was only trying to keep the North from conquering her. Whether she was mistaken or not, as she surely was, the South believed that she was fighting for life, and she was determined no hostile foot should remain on her soil; and when Gen. Pope did not go back fast enough Gen. Lee pressed after him and drove him to the banks of the Potomac. We fought our last battle in this compaign in Virginia in sight of the church spires of Alexandria—the battle of Chantilly—and then began a movement on Maryland. Moving up the Potomac, we crossed in Loudon beyond Leesburg, and took our first rest at Frederick, in Maryland.

Roger's letter to Helen gives us a full account of this march.

FREDERICK, MD., September, 1862.

My Dear Helen: We remained at the camp at Manassas only a day after I wrote, and then began our march up the Potomac. We came into Loudon County, a beautiful fertile country, in strange contrast with the desolate land we had left behind. We found in Loudon the most delightful people, who gave us genuine coffee, rich cream, golden butter, nice hams, and the other evidences of civilization. We were, however, on the move all the time. The other night in our march we had some real fun. Our chaplain, who is my great friend, is a young man full of life and activity. He bought a horse of uncertain age, after the battle of Manassas, whom he called "Old Rip." He made a pair of saddle pockets out of his knapsack, and stuffed a few clothes in them. He is always foraging for the rest of us. The other day he turned aside from the line of march and found where he could buy a chicken and some Irish potatoes. He prepared the chicken for the frying pan, and fried it himself as nicely as an inexperienced chaplain could, boiled the praties, and put the provisions in his haversack for papa and the others of our mess. When he reached us we were crossing Goose Creek. There was a temporary bridge over it for the infantry, but the horsemen had to ford. The ford was rough and rocky, and the horses plunged a good deal, but in went the daring chaplain. About the time he reached the deepest part Old Rip stepped on a stone and lost his footing and fell over on his side, and the poor chaplain went under head and ears. His knapsack saddlebags were soaked, and he was simply saturated. As he came out of the water John Baker in all sincerity called out: "Parson, are you wet?" The chaplain told him he thought so. There happened to be a fire near by, and he dried his damp garments and went on his way. When we got to the Potomac I noticed that he waded across like the rest of us and let another man ride Old Rip.

When we had crossed the Potomac we were in Maryland. The Marylanders, like the Virginians, are very warm in their Southern sympathies, and treated us very kindly. The Sunday bells were ringing when we pitched our camp in sight of the good old city of Frederick. Here we are to stay some days. I don't think Gen. Pope, whose headquarters are in the saddle, will be after us till he gets over the drubbing we gave him in Virginia. These Frederick people are mightily mixed: some of them very ardent Southerners, and some of them as ardent Unionists. I was really sorry for an old fellow who sold out his whole hardware stock for Confederate money, which certainly can't do him any good in buying a new supply of merchandise. I went to church Sunday afternoon; but the preacher was evidently scared at so many soldiers, for he did not preach. I found some very kind people here, and was very glad that nobody, Unionist or rebel, was molested by our people, but all was quiet and orderly.

I will write again as soon as I can. ROGER.

The army moved on from Frederick; but much to Roger's after surprise, there were ninety thousand Federals just behind it. The next letter of Roger's was some two weeks afterwards, and was from Virginia:

WARRENTON, VA., September 20, 1862.

My Dear Sister: Papa has telegraphed to you that I was wounded at South Mountain, but that I was not at all in any danger, and I hope your anxiety is at an end. We left Frederick and marched through a beautiful country and made our grand *entrée* into Hagerstown, four miles from the Pennsylvania line. We had no idea there were any yanks nearer than Washington City except a few cavalrymen who were skirmishing all the time with our boys; but we had scarcely got rested from our march before the command to march came, and we went down the same road we came up. As we marched we could hear the constant rattle of musketry and the boom of guns. We reached the foot of the South Mountain and saw Gen. Lee and Gen. Longstreet and Gen. Jones all together, and we marched on and took our place at the top of the mountain behind a stone wall. The cannons were shooting over our heads at some advancing Federals, whom we could not see. At length we were ordered forward, and as we crossed another stone fence and went into a wood, the bullets whizzed about us very sharply and one struck me on the neck, but just scratched me. We were firing as rapidly as we could at the enemy in our front, when I saw a man running to papa, who was commanding the regiment, and I saw him look around in alarm. We were enfiladed, and the enemy was just about to surround us entirely. Papa gave the order to retire, and we did so not a moment too soon, for they were nearly all around us. We entered the wood we had left, and were preparing to rally on the stone wall, when I felt a deadness in my left leg and fell to the ground. I thought my leg was torn off, but I looked and saw it was there still. Some of the boys put me on a stretcher and then in an ambulance. Poor papa came to me and saw how I was hurt, and said: "All right, boy, keep a brave heart. You shall have a furlough now." Well, I suffered a little, but not as much as many. The surgeon bandaged my leg as best he could and sent me in an ambulance with several others to the hospital here. I can't walk nor use a crutch yet, but I am getting along very well indeed. Miss Berta Phillips, a nice young lady, is going to take me to her home as soon as the doctor will let me go. I know there has been a battle at Sharpsburg since

I left the army, and I hope dear papa has come out safely. I know you have all heard ere this.

Give a great deal of love to everybody.

Affectionately,   Roger.

The battle of Sharpsburg was fought on Wednesday after the battle of South Mountain on Sunday. Col. Lawson led his regiment so gallantly that he was promoted to a brigadier general, and yet escaped without a serious wound.

CHAPTER XV.

"YANK" AND "JOHNNY" IN THE SAME HOSPITAL.

WHILE Roger was in the hospital at Warrenton a young Federal officer, who had been wounded in a cavalry fight at Brandy, and left in our lines, was brought to it. He had his elbow bone shivered by a pistol shot, and as the bullet plowed its way through the muscles of his arm it lacerated them badly, and made a very ugly wound. He and Roger soon became good friends. They were the same age, and had many experiences in common.

The young Federal was the son of a former Congressman from Connecticut, a Judge Bingham. In spite of his wound he was uniformly cheerful. But one morning when the surgeon looked at his wound his face grew serious. He saw a little speck of green which told of the deadly gangrene. The boy must be removed from the hospital, or death would likely come into it. He told Roger this, and Roger set to work to save his companion. Miss Berta Phillips was to come for him that morning; but he resolved that he would not go, or Bingham should go with him.

Miss Berta's bright face came beaming to the door: "I want my soldier boy."

"But I am not going."

"Why?"

"Because I want you to take somebody else. I am doing as well as I can do; but there is a little yank here who will die if somebody don't take him out from this place, and you must take him."

"Me take a yankee? No, sir!"

"Yes you will. You just see him, and you'll take him."

"Well, I won't see him."

"Yes you will."

"But I won't."

"Yes you will. Just listen: He has a good, sweet mother, and a pretty sister, and a good old father, and they are Presbyterians like you are, and he'll die if he don't get away."

"Well, can't I take you too?"

"Yes, I reckon so; but you must take him if you do."

"Well, I won't; but you may."

So Lieut. Bingham went with Roger to the delightful home of the Phillips family, where the comforts of life and tender watching of kind

friends soon expelled the poison from his veins.
But Roger must tell about the meeting:

PHILLIPS HOUSE, WARRENTON, VA., October, 1861.

Dear Helen: I am now in the sweetest old home in Virginia, the old Phillips mansion. Miss Berta came for me and brought me here, and with me brought my friend, and who do you reckon that friend is? A Connecticut yankee, a Federal lieutenant. Poor fellow! he got a terrible wound in his arm, and will never use it well again. He fell into our hands, and is a prisoner. He is a jolly, clever fellow, and as he and I were in the same ward in the hospital, we became good friends. He calls me "Johnny," and I call him "Yank." He can only use one hand, and I can only use one leg. So he helps me and I help him. He showed me his mother's picture, and his sister's too. His father used to be in Congress with Mr. Stephens, and has been a judge in his State. I think that they are rich people, and from what he says I am sure that they are very refined.

I am so glad that dear papa escaped, and I hear that he is recommended for a brigadier general's commission. I know that he deserves it, and I am sure that he will get it.

I am going to get a furlough soon, and if I can I am going to bring "Yank" with me. ROGER.

Sure enough Roger got his furlough, and through Mr. Stephens's influence Lieut. Bingham got a parole. He was permitted to go to Liberty County, in Georgia, and remain there till he was exchanged. I am glad to tell of this, for young folks are apt to think that where there is hard fighting there must be personal hate; but they are much mistaken. The Federals and Confederates never hated each other, and the soldiers of either side were always willing to help each other, and no people were more rejoiced when the war ended than those who fought it through. But I have some letters of the lieutenant's, in which he tells the story for himself:

"Pine Lodge," Liberty Co., Ga., October, 1862.

Hon. John H. Bingham, Binghamton, Conn.

My Honored Father: You have heard from me before doubtless, as I sent my letter through the lines just after I was captured. I am now at Gen. Lawson's, in Liberty County, Ga., on parole. As soon as I can be exchanged I will come home. I received the £20 bill of exchange before I left, and cashed it, and so am supplied with funds. Thank you. With love to all and high respect, I am

Yours,   John H. Bingham, Jr.

To his sister:

"Pine Lodge," Liberty County, Ga., November, 1862.

My Dear Clara: Such a series of adventures as I have had. It would be a real novel if it was written out. You see at Brandy, as we were making a charge, a Confed for whom I was going with my saber sent a pistol bullet through my bridle arm. My horse got away with me, and the first thing I knew I was in the midst of a battalion of Confederate cavalry. Of course I surrendered, and they were very kind to me. The surgeon bound up my wound and put me in the ambulance and sent me to Warrenton to the hospital. In the same ward with me was a young rebel. He is about my age and is as jolly as he can be. He and I struck up quite a friendship.

"Well, Yank," he said, "let's be partners. You've got no arm, and I have got no leg. You walk for me, and I'll cut for you."

"Agreed," I said, "Johnny, we'll shake on that, only I can't shake much now;" and so we "affiliated," as old Dr. Stiles used to say.

Well, we just told all about things at home. He has a smart sister, he says, and a good mother, and so have I. I like to have had to pass in my checks, for I was threatened with hospital gangrene, but Johnnie got me out of the hospital into a nice home, and Mr. Stephens got me a parole from the war office, so I did not have to go to Libby. And then Johnny said I must come home with him, and I got a permit to do it, and I am here.

You never saw anything like this delightful pine woods home. It is delightful now in November. The sky is so blue, the air is so balmy, and the woods are filled with flowers. I counted twenty-five different kinds yesterday. The family are Mrs. Lawson, a sweet lady about mother's age, and Miss Helen, who is older than you. I tell you she's a team. Talk about you yankee girls, she can beat you so far you can't see. There are two hundred and fifty negroes here to be fed and clothed and managed, and she is the head of all. True, she has an excellent manager and a faithful driver, but after all she is queen. I don't think she likes me much, because I am a yankee soldier, but I can't blame her for that. She treats me very kindly despite that. I hear I am to be exchanged next week, and I will come to Binghamton in a hurry.

Your brother　　　　　　　　　　　　　　　JOHN H., JR.

Roger's letter to his father tells how things were at "Pine Lodge:"

"PINE LODGE," November, 1862.

My Dear Papa: Jack came to us in good time. I am sorry he had to leave you, but I do not know how we could have done without him. Yank and I left Warrenton a week ago. His arm was still pretty bad, but the doctor thought that it was best for him to get to a milder climate, and he said I would be better off also.

The Phillipses were very kind to the last, and they furnished us with a good supply of nice things for our luncheons along the way. We came by Richmond. We had to change cars quite often; but Jack almost carried me in his arms, and without serious delay we reached Fleming. Helen had come to meet us, and she looked radiant in her new homespun and with her palmetto hat. She looked a little askance at poor Yank, but he was so pleasant he soon made a good friend of her. We came in good time to "Pine Lodge," and found mother waiting for us. Old Jack met us and Mammy came as fast as the poor old soul could, and Yank's eyes opened when she threw her arms around me and cried like a baby.

I was not hurt by the trip at all, and have been improving every day. So has Yank. He had a letter from his father through the lines, sent through commissioners for the exchange of prisoners, inclosing him a £20 Bank of England note, which he turned into Confederate money at Richmond, so his wants were supplied. He is very much interested and pleased with what he sees. He is a nice fellow, and while I can't make him see that we are right, and don't try very hard, he sees in how many things he has been mistaught. The negroes, especially the little fellows in the quarters, keep him continually amused. I will be sorry when he goes, as he says he must next week. He is to report at Savannah and be exchanged at Port Royal.

Things are going about as well as we could hope for. Mr. Jones has managed admirably. He has moved all the negro families from Medway and "Lawson Place," and keeps there only a gang of hands who are harvesting the rice. We made a pretty good crop, which Mr. Harris writes us is already sold to the government. We are having it shipped as fast as it can be brought to Fleming.

Mamma is quite well, as you see from her letter. I am getting along only middling. The bone which was broken was splintered a little, and the wound does not heal rapidly. I can only get about with my crutches I am very thankful that it it is as well with me though, you may be sure. I am glad to hear you have the three stars and are now a general. I hope you will give me a place on your staff.

Ever affectionately, ROGER.

The winter came, and the battle of Fredericksburg was fought, but Roger could not get back to the army in time to engage in it. He, however, continued to improve, and in February he was enabled to report for duty, and received this pleasant communication from the war office:

WAR OFFICE.

Serg. Maj. Lawson, of the Seventy-fifth Regiment, Georgia troops, is hereby promoted for gallantry on the field, and is commissioned as Second Lieut., C. S. A. He will report for duty to Brig. Gen. Lawson, Jones's Division, Longstreet's Corps, A. N. V. A. R. TAPE, A. A. A. G.

SPECIAL ORDER NO. 750.

Lieut. Roger Lawson is hereby assigned for staff duty on the staff of Brig. Gen. Lawson, Army Northern Virginia.

A. R. TAPE, A. A. A. G.

So he returned to the army and began his work in the early spring.

CHAPTER XVI.

THE ARMY AGAIN—WINTER QUARTERS.

THE flowers were blooming when Roger left "Pine Lodge" for Virginia; the snow was on the ground when he reached the camp at Guineas Station. There was no fighting, save a little skirmishing now and then. The attention of the enemy was turned to Vicksburg and the western army, and Gen. Lee was having a little rest.

Roger found himself in a new position, and was able to write home very often. Some of his letters give a picture of a camp in winter quarters. They had pitched their camp in a wood, where they could get shelter and fuel, and whiled away the time as profitably and as pleasantly as they could. The victory at Marye Heights, near Fredericksburg, in December had been purchased at no small cost of men, and the new recruits who came in were being drilled as diligently as possible to take the places of the missing. Save to keep everything in trim for the movements in the spring, neither Federals nor Confederates were doing much. The officers who could be spared were on furlough, and Gen. Lawson had gone to Liberty for a two weeks' stay. Roger wrote them all in writing to Helen:

CAMP LEE, January, 1863.

My Dear Helen: I knew that I ought not to stay at home any longer, but it was a great trial for me to leave you all. I had spent so many pleasant hours at "Pine Lodge" that it was hard for me to tear myself away.

The more I see of war, the more I hate it. When will people learn to settle their difficulties like Christians? As we are in it, we must go through with it, and I must try and do my duty.

I reached here safely, just stopping long enough in Richmond to order me a lieutenant's dress uniform, which only cost me a thousand dollars. I don't expect to use it a great deal. I reported at headquarters. Our brigade headquarters are in an old house overlooking the wood where the brigade is camped. It is comfortable enough for old soldiers, as we are getting to be. Our fare is not the most elegant; but Jack is not a bad forager, and we get along pretty well. The troops are busy drilling and attending carefully to camp routine. We have our dress parades every evening, and sometimes our camp is enlivened by the faces of the wives of some of the officers of the Virginia soldiers. All kinds of fun is kept agoing. We have games of ball and racing, and music of all kinds, from the old time fiddle to the modern band. Whenever we have a snow there is a regular snow battle. The troops are drawn up in regular line. They establish batteries, put out skirmishers, and have regular fusillades. The victors roll the conquered in the snow. But the thing that I most enjoy is the revival. We have preaching every night. Some of the best men of all the Churches preach for us. We have a Y. M. C. A., and I joined it as soon as I returned. We have regular camp meeting times. Mr. Lester, the Chaplain of the Third Georgia; Mr. Jarrell, of the Eighteenth Georgia; Mr. Dodge and Mr. Thigpen, of Colquitt's Brigade, are some of our Methodist chaplains; and Messrs. Curry and MacCallum are Baptists. Bishop Pierce came to see his son, and spent several days in camp; and Bishop Elliot, of the Episcopal Church, gave us a glorious sermon. Then we have old Dr. Stiles and Dr. Hoge, of the Presbyterian Church; and Dr. Jeter and Dr. Jones, of the Baptist Church; and a host of others. They have glorious singing in the meetings, and some are converted at every service, and the Church doors are opened, and the soldiers say what Church they wish to belong to.

Of course there is a great deal of wickedness in camp. Many of our officers and men are very bad; but there is a great deal of good. Our grand old general is always at service, and no one ever thinks of his doing anything which one ought not to do. As to old Jack, we all know how good he is. Gen. Colquitt talks to his men and prays for them like a preacher, and Gen. Gordon is always ready to help in the meetings.

I know that it is right hard to be good in camp. It is so hard to find a place to pray; but I am glad that my tent mate, who is an Episcopalian—Maj. Lanford—prays night and morning. He tries to live right, though he will say bad words sometimes when he gets fretted. He says that he means no harm by it, though.

We have a capital set of fellows on our staff. Maj. Middleton, our quartermaster, is from an old South Carolina family, and is a man of fine education and excellent mind. He is the jolliest fellow in the world—always in a good humor. He has taken quite a fancy for me, and laughs at me for being a Methodist; but I know that he is glad that I don't drink or gamble.

But I have little to write now. Love to all. ROGER.

There are few things more monotonous than the life of the camp when there is no enemy near, and the early days of 1863 were uneventful and wearisome. The Federals were getting in new recruits, and the conscripting of the whole South was sending new men into the army to be made ready for service. It became evident to even the common soldier as May drew on that there was something about to happen of serious kind; and so there was, for the battle of Chancellorsville was fought. The Confederates won the battle; but at what a fearful cost! for Stonewall Jackson was killed, alas! by his own men, through a fearful mistake. The brigade to which Roger belonged, which had been so fearfully cut up at the fight in December, was not brought into this action, and he had little to write except concerning the sad event which so distressed the whole South:

CAMP LEE, May, 1862.

My Dear Helen: You have heard the sad news. Gen. Jackson is dead! You cannot imagine the shadow that it has thrown over the whole army. Dear old "Jack," as we used to call him, so quiet and calm and determined, so courteous to everybody, so pious, so brave. It would have been sad enough for him to have been killed leading his own corps to battle, but to fall by a shot from one who would have died for him was too sad. Gen. Lee, always so calm, has an air of deep grief which is indescribable. The victory that we have won is not a victory, now that Jackson is dead.

We are getting ready now for a move northward. Of course we do not know where we are going, but from the nature of the going to take the offensive, and I would not be at all surprised if we find ourselves in Pennsylvania before the campaign ends. Gen. Lee is anxious to end this thing.

Mr. Lincoln, you know, has issued his proclamation, and the negroes are as free as he can make them, and we are now as strong as we will ever be. If old Jack were at the head of his corps, I would not be troubled; but alas! he is not there, and there is no one to take his place. We have just received orders to move, and I do not know when I can write you again.

ROGER.

It was a long time before he did write again. Gen. Lee did advance, as he supposed that he would. The battle of Gettysburg was fought, and among the wounded and missing as reported in the lists was Lieut. Roger Lawson, A. A. G., of Lawson's Brigade.

CHAPTER XVII.

THE AMERICAN WATERLOO.

I HAVE never been able to read without a shudder the story of Gettysburg, and those who wish to hear of the terrible events of those awful days must go elsewhere to find them told than to these pages. I only know that when the few came back from that daring and magnificent but fatal charge on the second day, when the hundred guns poured out their volleys of shot and shell, Roger Lawson was not one of them; and when Brig. Gen. Lawson gathered up the remnants of his brigade for the retreat to Maryland he had to leave his own son behind. A flag of truce, however, brought him the news that Roger, with a shattered arm, was a prisoner; that his wound, though serious, was not mortal. Gen. Lawson himself had his horse shot under him and received a slight wound, or what appeared then to be a slight one, in his chest, but was not so disabled as not to be able to handle his brigade. He wrote to his wife:

Near GETTYSBURG, July, 1863.

only know Gen. Lee said, "Charge the guns;" and we went for them. The men never behaved better, and our boy swept over the field as long as it was possible for a man to sit on his horse, as calmly as he ever led a chase at home. As we climbed the heights it was no longer possible to remain on horseback, and he leaped from the saddle, and sword in hand led the men toward the guns. I lost sight of him in the terrible struggle. We broke through the line, we captured the guns, but before we could make our victory sure the Federal reserve came on, and a new battery poured a deadly fire upon us, and the order came to retire. I did not know what had become of my boy, save that Capt. Barclay said he saw him fall, until this morning, when I received this note by flag of truce:

HOSPITAL CAMP, U. S A.

Gen. Lawson: Your son, Lieut. Lawson, is in our hands and under my care in the hospital. He begs me to say he is not mortally wounded; his right arm is shattered and he may lose it, but his life is safe. He will receive all the care we can possibly give him.

Yours, THOMAS MCLEAN, *Asst. Sur. U. S. A.*

I telegraphed you that he was wounded and a prisoner, but safe. I am expecting every moment for the brigade to move southward, but I can send this by one of the cavalry who is going to Virginia to-night. ROGER LAWSON.

Roger was removed to the hospital in the little city of Gettysburg. There was no hope for his right arm, which had been almost cut off by a shell, and it was decided to amputate it at once. His first letter was to his mother and was written by an amanuensis:

GETTYSBURG HOSPITAL, July, 1863.

My Darling Mother: As you see, my handwriting is improved. The fact is I have got into the good graces of a nice little Pennsylvania maiden, and she is writing for me. I am glad I am able to dictate a letter, for I tell you it looked once like I never would write or speak again. Before I went into battle I raised my heart to God, and as we went into that storm of shot and shell I knew no more until I fell. The brigade was repulsed. I lay on the field for several hours. Some kind Federal going over the battlefield saw me unable to move, for my old wound had left my leg so weak that in trying to mount the heights, just as the shot struck my arm I fell and sprained my ankle; they took me in their arms and carried me to a camp fire, where one of them gave me some coffee and some hard-tack. I had eaten nothing all day, and when I took the coffee and bread I was refreshed. By this time the ambulance corps was coming nigh, and one, an honest-looking "Buckeye," said: "Say, lieutenant, you have a gold watch, I see. If you go to the hospital with it on, it is likely you'll never see it again. Now give it to me, and give me your name and address, and I will take care of it for you and send it home to your folks as soon as I get a chance."* The fellow looked so honest that I did not care to help myself if I could, and I could not if I would, so I handed it over. Maybe you'll get it or hear of it; likely not.

Well, mamma, don't be troubled about me. I am all right. The doctor cut off my arm just above the elbow, but he says I am doing splendidly. God has been very good to me, and these good people of the Christian Commission are kind and considerate. I do not know where I'll go after I leave here, but I am likely to stay here some time yet. I know I can't go anywhere that your prayers won't follow me and God will not be near me.

I see in the daily papers that my old friend Bingham was distinguished for his gallantry, and has been promoted to a captaincy. I am glad to hear of it. God bless you.

Ever your boy, ROGER.

---

*And he did. The watch came safely as soon as communication was restored.

CHAPTER XVIII.

HOSPITAL LIFE.

THE sprained ankle kept Roger in bed, as the severed arm necessarily kept him in his ward. Many people came to the hospital. They came from all sections of the North, and of course Roger had all kinds of visitors. Of these some were very agreeable, and some otherwise.

The persistence with which the people of the United States have misunderstood and misrepresented each other is certainly a strange fact in our history, and nothing is more unwelcome to either section than a true story of the character of the people of the opposition. Now I am sure that, Southern born as I am, and Southern bred, and with nearly all my readers in the South, I should gratify many of them much more than I will if I were to say that all Northern people were unscrupulous, malignant, cruel, and all Southerners were generous, forgiving, tender. I am sure that those people who look upon "Uncle Tom's Cabin" as authentic history will not be apt to accept such an account as this of Helen and Roger as a true one. Well, I can't help that; I know the mass of the Northern people were honest in their belief that they were fighting for liberty, and many of them kindly in their feelings toward their misguided foes of the South; and I know that just such people as Roger and Helen were found now, and then in all the South, but if I were to leave the impression that there were no other kind of folks, North or South, I certainly would mislead; and Roger found this to be true, much to his annoyance.

The Federal army was well provided with everything, and no two parts of its equipment were more valuable and praiseworthy than the Christian and sanitary commissions. The battle of Gettysburg was no sooner over than both were on the ground, and in providing for the wounded they knew no distinction of uniforms; blue and gray were alike objects of care. The good women of Gettysburg were, as good women are everywhere, full of kindly sympathies, and a genial old maid took Roger, rebel as he was, under her especial care. She wrote his letters for him, brought him books to read, and prepared nice dishes for him. She came to see him every day. She was a great Unionist, but she took her "wicked rebel," as she called Roger, under her careful charge; but there were other visitors who did not look so kindly on him. They came to his cot, and when they found out he was a rebel they looked as if some awful wrong had been done them by the government taking care of him at all, and hurried on. It was not often they said anything, but one day a very smooth, oily, quick-spoken visitor from Massachusetts came through the hospital. He was gushing over the brave defenders of the flag, and copiously pouring out his words of commendation. When he came to Roger's cot he evidently thought him a Federal soldier, and said: "Ah! my poor hero, you have, I see, given up your own brave right arm in defense of our flag. What regiment was yours?"

"I was a Confederate, sir."

"What? *you* a rebel?"

"No, sir; a Confederate soldier."

"No, sir! You were a rebel against the best government the world ever saw. You lost your arm, and you ought to have lost your head," he said angrily.

"And you *have* lost yours, you dirty coward!" said the surgeon, who had just come up. "You get out of this ward, or I will make the hospital steward kick you out."

"Why, Captain"—

"Not a word more, sir. No man shall be insulted in this hospital by any one, much less by a coward who does not dare to fight for his principles. Leave here, sir, leave." And he left.

But this was not half so annoying as an encounter he had with a good woman from Western New York. She came to his cot, and said softly, and with apparent great sincerity, when she knew who he was: "Well, my young friend, I hope you are prepared to die."

"Yes, I hope so, ma'am; but I am in no special hurry to do so."

"I learn you are a rebel."

"Yes, ma'am; some call us so."

"Well, I hope, my young friend, that the severe chastisement visited on you has led you to repentance."

"I fear not, ma'am."

"There are none so hopeless as those that are hardened in sin. You have been fearfully guilty, and your sin has found you out."

"And ef you plase, ma'am," said the Irish soldier who was in charge, " ef you plase, ma'am, the docther says we were not to parmit the visitors to talk too much to the patients."

"Well, I will obey his orders, but my conscience bids me to say, young man, that ' He that being often reproved hardeneth his neck, shall suddenly be destroyed, and that without remedy.'"

She walked majestically away with the sweet complacency of one who had done her full duty.

Roger was nervous and sad and lonely, and the cold, hard, metallic tone of the woman's voice hurt him more than he was willing to admit. Just then Miss Alice, his good friend, came to make her daily visit. She saw the shadow over his face, and asked him what was the matter, why he looked so sad?

"O, nothing," he said, with a faint smile.

"Yis, mom, if yez had been here whin that lady phats just gone out was a preachin' to the Lieutenant, an' callin' him a rebel an' what not, yez wouldn't be shurprized at the way he luks."

"O yes, I know her; and I am determined you shan't have this bother any longer. If Dr. McLean will help me (and I think he will), we will have you moved to the Confederate hospital, and there you will be free from annoyance."

When she spoke to the doctor, and told him of the disagreeable visitors, he readily promised to do as she wished, and added: "If they come about that old copperhead, Dr. Sims, they will catch it certain. The peppery old fellow is an old army surgeon, and is not hurt by his loyalty anyhow. Yes, I'll move the Lieutenant to-morrow."

So Roger was moved. It was some weeks before he could walk. The old wound broke out again, and the old doctor insisted on an operation, to which Roger cheerfully submitted. Then Roger began rapidly to recover, and was soon almost well. Miss Alice was as kind as she had always been, but, like many good people, she was poor, and Roger had no money and only such clothing as the hospital supplied, and he was in no condition to leave it.

One day a Maryland lady visited the hospital with supplies from Baltimore for the Confederates. As she left Roger, after a pleasant visit, she put in his hand this card: "Write to your sister, Mrs. Charles Bacon, and let her know your needs." This was all. When Miss Alice came she saw the card. "That's the very thing," she said. "I know both Lizzie Bacon and her husband, and I know they are willing and able to help any of her kin, but I did not know she was your sister."

"And she is not, unless she is a Methodist; for I have but one sister, and that is Helen."

" Well, she is a Methodist, and as you are not permitted to get help except some from your relations, I reckon you might call her sister."

"Well, I must have some help, and so you may write to her for me." And Miss Alice took her pencil and wrote as Roger dictated. He asked for a loan of $50, to be returned as soon as he had reached home. In a week a check for $50 was received in a short note signed simply, "Your Sister Lizzie."

In those days when every act was carefully watched and detectives were in every corner and every offer of help to a Southern soldier was looked upon with suspicion, this somewhat innocent form of deception was not unusual nor looked upon with any special disfavor, nor did the Federal officers inquire very closely as to the facts.

An overcoat and a plain suit of gray, purchased with a part of the money, supplied Roger with clothing, but he had no money left. Miss Alice, however, Union woman as she was, moved among the Southern sympathizers, who were not a few in Pennsylvania, and Roger went well furnished to Fort Delaware, where he was regularly enrolled as a prisoner. He managed to get several short, cheery letters through the lines which brought relief to the burdened hearts at "Pine Lodge."

CHAPTER XIX.

"PINE LODGE" AGAIN.

IF I did not give my young readers frequent glimpses of home life in these trying days, I should very sadly fail in my purpose, which is to show how the days through which the whole country passed in these years of conflict developed character. The men who were old enough to fight were ordered to the front, and upon the women and older men and children fell all the burden of providing for those at home and in the army.

The cutting off of the interior of the country from all foreign supplies made it necessary for everything to be produced at home. Mr. Jones had decided that after the rice crop of 1863 was harvested it would be impossible to make another, and so he had removed all the negroes from the coast to the pine woods. The home guard kept up a constant patrol and protected the farms which were out of reach of the gunboats. Those on the rivers were abandoned. There were no Federal forces nearer than Port Royal and Fort Pulaski, but the island and the coast were exposed to attack and devastation at any time. The necessity of the times led the planters to turn everything in the direction of food production.

Helen had been director general of everything at "Pine Lodge," but Mr. Jones now relieved her and took charge of the large plantation. Still she had much to do, and did what no one thought she could do. Her father was more than ever concerned about home, and Helen wrote him very fully of what she was trying to have done:

December, 1863.

My Dear Papa: As you suggested, Mr. Jones decided to move everything from "Lawson Place" and Medway, and for the time abandon any effort to plant another crop of rice. He has rented four hundred acres of his brother's place, and expects to plant the swamp field in upland rice. We expect to put twenty acres in potatoes, and forty acres in ground peas for the hogs. All the newly cleared land we will put in peas. I had five acres in turnips, and with one of our large sirup kettles we managed to make a good soup for the little negroes every day. Our potato crop was good, and they are keeping well and help us out greatly. We find that while we cannot feed the people like we did, yet they have an abundance of rice and potatoes and sirup. We manage to supply them with meat at least twice a week. I write you this particularly, because I know you are so interested in these facts.

Young Bob and Stumpy Bill ran away and were caught by the home guard and brought home. You know Bob has a wife and eight children, and Bill has a family as large. They expected me to turn them over for punishment to Mr. Jones, but I said to them: "Now, boys, if you want to go to the yankees, *go;* but you must take your families. If you can take care of them better than we can, take them. I am willing. I am not going to have Mr. Jones punish you, but I don't want to see you on this place after to-night unless you are going to behave properly, and the first time you do wrong again I am going to drive you and your families off the place." They were very penitent, and I don't think will leave again.

We heard from Roger. He could only write a line. He was cheerful and well. Mamma sends much love. HELEN.

The people at home were put up to all they could do, but the South is so generous in her gifts to the laborer that subsistence is only impossible to the absolutely idle. They had no flour, but they had rice. The rice mills were out of reach, and they pounded the rice in mortars. The wax myrtle and tallow gave them candles. The sugar cane patch gave them sugar and sirup. The cotton fields gave them material for clothing. The negroes could not get leather for shoes, but the climate was so mild they did not need them. The old women carded cotton and wool, and the young women spun it and wove it into cloth, and so the little colony was supplied; and one-tenth of all was sent to the army to help to supply it with stores.

Helen still attended her Sunday school regularly, and still managed it almost alone. The good mother bore the burden of unceasing anxiety, but lived in the atmosphere of trust and prayer. The few neighbors who were left were very kind, and did what they could to help, but the burdens fell on all alike.

CHAPTER XX.

PRISON LIFE.

THERE is little pleasure to me in telling of anything connected with the fratricidal strife between the States; but sad as it was, it was—and we need not try (for we cannot do so) to blot the story out. But of all its chapters there are none which to me are so painful as those that tell of prison life. It is impossible to make such a life agreeable, but, alas! many things were done and left undone by both sides to make it worse than it ought to have been, and then, perhaps, partisan hate has added to the story its usual exaggerations. I do not think it is a fit thing for either side to reproach the other. For every act of oppression in Andersonville or Libby Prison a like act just as indefensible can be found in Elmira and Fort Delaware and Johnson's Island. Why prisoners were not exchanged and much suffering avoided is a question we need not open here, but when Roger came to Fort Delaware the exchange had ceased, and there was nothing before him but to wait till the end.

There had been, as there always is in times of war, questions about the treatment of prisoners which each side answered to suit itself; and in order to punish the guilty, the two governments decided to punish the innocent. They called this retaliation, and it was sufficiently cruel and diabolical to be called anything, and to both governments was a blot of darkest dye.

Fort Delaware was now under the charge of a brutal German named Schoef, who was willing to go beyond even his orders in punishing the poor prisoners under his charge. On a little island, a treeless sand bed in the Delaware bay where the Brandywine empties into it, was this large fort, intended as a defense to the city of Philadelphia, sixty miles away. On this island barracks had been erected. They were of thin boards, hot in summer and fearfully cold in winter. Here the prisoners were divided into companies and messes and placed under guard. The officers were in one set of barracks and the privates in another. The whole was in command of the German colonel and the various companies under the command of subalterns. Escape was almost impossible, for deep water was on every side. The officers in the barracks were divided into messes, and were furnished from the commissary department with a meager supply of unpalatable food, and in winter a very small quantity of fuel and a very limited amount of clothing and bedding. The prisoners made the best of the situation. They had religious services, gave concerts, had court for the trial of offenders, had their trading booths, sold fried rats, catfish, and ginger cake, and, alas! gambled in every possible way.

The details of personal suffering and needless cruelty at last came to the ears of Col. Thruston, Member of Congress from Ohio, whose nephew was in prison. He had an interview with Mr. Lincoln. The kindly heart of the President was much moved by his story of the sufferings of the prisoner, and he sent for Mr. Stanton. When the Secretary came he told him what he had heard and told him to order the officer commanding to abate his rigorous treatment. "Now, Mr. Secretary, the war is awful enough, and these deluded people are suffering enough without any needless cruelty, and I want you to detail some young American officers and put them in charge of the prisoners, good men and firm men, but not tyrants." The Secretary was in no very good humor; but the matter was settled; and so Capt. Bingham, of the Eleventh Connecticut, was ordered to report at the fort and assist in the work of caring for the prisoners.

When he looked over the list of prisoners committed to his charge he was startled to see the name of his old associate in the hospital at Warrenton. As soon as all his office affairs had been properly settled, he called his orderly and giving him a card with the name of Lieut. Roger Lawson on it, he gave him an order to request that Confederate officer to report at headquarters. Roger did not know the new commandant, and was much puzzled at the request, but at once accompanied the orderly. He was taken into the presence of the Captain.

"You can now retire, orderly, and close my door, and allow no one to disturb me for half an hour."

The orderly gave his salute and took his place at the door.

Roger did not at first recognize his friend. The pale-faced youth of two years before, dressed then in citizen's clothes, and the bronzed, mustached, uniformed soldier of to-day were not much alike. The Captain rose, and stepping to the door locked it, and quickly removed his coat. He stretched out a bare arm, and simply said: "See that, Johnny?"

A bright smile crossed the face of the prisoner as he stretched out his left hand and grasped the extended. "Yes, Yank; and I am glad to see you had better luck than I did."

The two friends had a royal time for the half-hour, and then Capt. Bingham said to his friend: "Now, Johnny, you know how I am situated, but anything I can do for you I will do. If you choose to take a place in the commissary department, I can give it to you."

"No, I am obliged to you. I prefer not to leave my messmates, but I am as grateful to you as if I were to accept your kindness."

"Well, I don't blame you for not leaving them. I am aware of some things here which need correction, and you can assure your fellow-prisoners that while I will strictly regard orders from headquarters I will do all I can to prevent any abuse of them."

The half-hour was soon gone. As Roger rose to go his friend handed him five crisp ten-dollar greenbacks and said: "Take this as a loan."

Roger hesitated; but, remembering that it was foolish pride that would not allow a friend to do a favor for one when he was in need, he accepted.

There was no indication when the Captain inspected the camp and came to the company of which Roger was one that he knew the prisoner;

nor did Roger allow any one to know that the captain in charge was his friend.

He still kept up his correspondence with Miss Alice and Mrs. Bacon. Among his associate prisoners was Gen. Forney, of Alabama. He had known Gen. Lawson in the army, and soon had a tender regard for his son. One day he said to him: "Lawson, study law. Get a 'Blackstone' and I'll be your preceptor."

"Agreed," said Roger.

So "Blackstone" with other books was secured from Judge Bingham's through his son, and Roger began his studies. Months came and went. The daily papers told of Gen. Grant's persistent and futile efforts to get to Richmond, of the fall of Atlanta, and the siege of Petersburg; and poor Roger like a caged lion had to hear the story and feel the vain longing to be where he could do something for the cause.

CHAPTER XXI.

WAVE UPON WAVE.

THE lines of Grant were getting nearer and nearer to Richmond, but the grand generalship of Lee had kept the great captain who had won in every other field still out of the Confederate capital. Gen. Lawson's brigade was in front of Gen. Butler, who was mining away under the intrenchment which he could not carry by assault. The prisoners at Fort Delaware, comprising some of the brightest officers of the army, were still making the best of the situation. Roger was still diligently at work on his law books, and Gen. Forney was giving him careful instructions. Every month he received a letter without signature, inclosing ten dollars. The mess table was now well spread; and but for the terrible suspense and the exile from home the life of the imprisoned officers would have been tolerable. They received the New York and Philadelphia papers every day, and kept up with the news from the front. On the 1st of August, when the *Philadelphia Press* was brought to the camp, Roger saw in blazing headlines: "The mine sprung. Terrific slaughter of Confederates, Heavy loss of Federals. Overpowered by numbers, the Federals retire. Gen. Lawson, rebel brigadier, killed on the field." The heart of the poor fellow sunk, and he fell on his cot with his face buried in his pillow. Gen. Forney stood kindly by and finally laid his hand on his shoulder and said: "Lawson, this news may not be true. I doubt if it is. It is not likely that the reporter could have known certainly. Don't give up hope."

The orderly came at that moment. "Order for Lieut. Lawson from the Captain," he said.

Roger rose and wiped the tears from his eyes and accompanied the orderly.

When they were alone Capt. Bingham said: "Roger, there is no certainty in this report. Wait till you hear more directly. I have a friend on Butler's staff. I will wire him, and he will be able to remove your doubt. Cheer up and hope on."

It was about nightfall when the same orderly came with the same order, and when Roger reached his friend's office he handed him a dispatch:

Flag of truce just returned. Gen. Lawson not dead; wounded severely, but not fatally. JENKS.

The mail a few days later brought a letter from

his father through the flag of truce. It told him that his father was wounded in the shoulder, and that he would be disabled from service for some time; that he would return home on leave of absence.

The heart of the noble son rose in gratitude to God as he carried the good news to the affectionate friends of his mess.

Gen. Lawson left for home a week after he was wounded, and reached "Pine Lodge" safely. The wound he had received was severe, but not dangerous; and while it kept him confined to his house, it did not prevent him from attending to his business matters, which had become complicated during his long absence. He realized that matters were drawing toward a crisis, and perhaps there was to be an end which was not looked for. For years his overseer had left in his hands the money he did not need for expenses, and during these three years he had received no salary. The General had not been willing to offer him Confederate money, depreciated currency as it was, in payment of a debt incurred when gold and silver were the standards, and so the matter was unsettled. After he had been at home for two weeks he sent for his overseer, and said to him: "Mr. Jones, we have had no settlement since the war began, and it is time we are having one."

"Well, General, I hain't worried about that. I am willing for it to go on as it has been a gwine."

"No. I don't know how this war is going to end, and I do not know, if I get over this wound and get back to the army, but that I'll be less fortunate next time. I have no gold, I will not pay you in Confederate money, and I don't wish to leave you unsecured. I owed you at the beginning of the war $1,000 in gold. Your salary has been $500 a year, and there are three years unpaid. This will, with the interest, make about $3,000 I owe you now—just what this place cost. I am going to give you a deed to it. If I live, and things go right, I will pay you in good money after the war, or when you wish it, but I would feel better to know you were secure now."

"Well, suit yourself, General. I hain't scairt any way. I know you'll do right, and ef you go up we is all gone up."

The papers were drawn and the deed put on record. The skies grew darker. Sherman started in November on his march to the sea. There was no one to oppose him, as he well knew when he began it. He ravaged as he marched, and desolation remained behind him. It was evident that he aimed to strike the Atlantic and Gulf railroad as he had done the Central and Georgia, and destroy it as he had done the others. It was not likely, if the army came near "Pine Lodge," that they would fail to visit it. Gen. Lawson was in no condition to fly anywhere. The blow he had received on the chest at Gettysburg had left him with a cough which was sometimes alarming, and his wound had not healed rapidly. Roger's imprisonment, the unhappy condition of public affairs, the necessities of his people who had to be provided for, had burdened him greatly and retarded his recovery. When he had reason to expect a visit from the yankees, he called old Jack into his confidence. The old man was to keep guard and let him know when the yankees were in sight. Young Jack was to keep his horse always ready for him, and a place of refuge was to be provided in the swamp, and a bridleway made to it, and a palmetto-covered tent made for his protection. There were none, save Helen and her mother, old Jack and young Jack, who knew of this provision. Bob, the butler, was a favorite and trusted servant; and the General, with Bob and old Jack, went out into the pine wood back of the house and carefully buried a trunk containing valuable papers, the jewels, and the family plate.

The Federals drew nearer and nearer. The main army went down the Central road and a detachment of cavalry came through Liberty. Old Jack was at work in the field when he saw the bluecoats coming toward the house. He came out to the fence to meet them. They were so accustomed to glad greetings from the negroes, who looked upon them as their deliverers from bondage, that they were not at all surprised at the warm greeting of the old man: "Well, massa, you's here at las'. I's been lookin' fur you long time. Heap niggahs round here look fur you."

"Who is your master?"

"My master? Yes, sar, he named Mr. William Barnwell Smith, sir."

"Is there a Gen. Lawson living near here?"

"O yes, sar; Gen. Lawson lib down dat road about tree mile, sah. He be home. I seed him yisterday."

"Why, I thought they told us this was the way to his house."

"No, massa, I know de way. I go up to de house and git my mule. I go wid you and show you where he lib."

"Well, be quick about it."

"Yes, Massa; I be back in tree minute."

So Jack ran to the house. His master knew, as he saw him running, what it meant, and he was out of the back door, and in a full gallop to the swamp, in a moment. Young Jack dashed away on a horse in the other direction. He had on a gray coat, and when the Federals caught sight of him they put out in pursuit. He stopped as they fired the first shot, and they brought him to the captain. "Who do you belong to, sir?"

"Gin. Lawson, sah."

"Where does he live?"

"Right up dar, sah."

"Is he at home?"

"No, sah; he ain't been at home dese tree weeks."

"You lie, sir; he was at home this morning."

"Well, sah; maybe so. I ain't seen him."

"Where were you going?"

"Going to find de Unions, and git free."

"Where is that old nigger who said he would be back in three minutes?"

"O, dat old fool Jack? He don't know his own massa."

"Well, you take us to your master's."

"Yes, sah; dis way."

The negroes heard that the yankees had come, and they came running to meet them; Lean Bill, Stumpy Tom, Yellow Dick, and all the hosts. Old Aunt Judy and Mammy did not stir, and old Jack was nowhere to be found; but young Jack was the most delighted of all the gang. The bird had flown. The captain of the raiders came in. He was courteous to the ladies, but he was anxious to capture the brigadier. " Gen. Lawson lives here?"

" Yes, sir."
" Is he at home?"
" No, sir."
" Where is he?"
" I do not know, sir."
" When was he here last?"
" I decline to tell."
" I must search the house."
" Certainly, sir; you can do so."

The search was thorough. A search for new horse tracks was made, and they were in abundance, but they went every way. Old Jack was too wary to be caught that easy. At last they prepared to leave. They had all the stock gathered up (horses, mules, cows, calves, and everything that could be driven), and then told all the negroes who wished to go that they could go to the camp or elsewhere, and then left. Most of the negroes went, and, to the sorrow and astonishment of the mistress, the most delighted were young Jack and Bob.

That night some of the troopers, after they had

given Bob a good supper and several drinks of whisky from their canteens, took him aside, and said: "Now, my friend, if you want to make some money, tell us where you hid your master's money, and we'll divide with you."

"Well, sah; I don't know as how Mas Roger buried no money, but he buried a trunk; what he got in 'em I dunno."

"Can you find it?"

"Yes, sah; I specks so."

"Well, now, don't you tell nobody; you go with us there."

"Yes, sah."

So at midnight they went for the buried treasure. The faithful Bob took them to the spot where he had assisted in burying the trunk. *It was not there!* The troopers cursed him and kicked him and threatened to kill him, but he said truly he did not know where the trunk was. They could see that it had been there, and became convinced that he was not playing them false. The general was safe in his hiding place, and old Jack had made provision for what might come. He had a bed of pine straw, a warm supper of fried meat and corn hoecake, and kept watch while his wounded master rested. He knew the house would be watched, and he made himself invisible. At midnight of the second night he glided up to his cabin to tell his old wife the news to take to her mistress. It was two weeks before the last of the cavalry was gone, and during that time the General only left his lodging at midnight. "Lawson Place" was burned to the ground. There was only left some rough rice and potatoes for the negroes. The most of them went to the camp, but many of them returned after the raiders left; one who came back brought a few pounds of coffee for "ole miss." Bob, the traitor, never came back, but Jack came up with two good mules he had stolen from the yankees. The rice cut from the uplands was not yet threshed, and when the negroes returned all hands were put to gathering potatoes, threshing rice, and picking ground peas. There was a quantity of cowpeas still ungathered in the fields, and some cattle and hogs in the swamp which the raiders failed to get; and that supply, with a few bags of long cotton which were hidden away and which they did not find, was all that was left.

CHAPTER XXII.

FREE AT LAST.

THE march of Sherman toward the sea was duly heralded by the Northern press, and when he reached Savannah the full story of his wonderful exploit was told in flaming letters. Without a single regiment of veteran soldiers to oppose him, he had marched triumphantly to the coast. The story of homes devastated, of plantations ravaged, slaves freed, stock captured, houses burned, railways torn up, was pleasant reading in these wild times to the people of the North, who had begun to fear that the war would never end.

As poor Roger read these accounts he was miserable. He knew that the army must have struck the Atlantic and Gulf railroad not far from where his father's home was. But had his father been captured? What had become of his mother and Helen? The anxiety told upon him, and his noble foe could not but see it. So Capt. Bingham resolved that if it was in his power to get Roger released on parole it should be done. He knew that his father and Mr. Lincoln were great friends, and he felt assured that all Mr. Lincoln could do he would do. So he wrote to his father. He told of how Roger in all probability had saved his life, of how seriously he had been injured, and of the needlessness of keeping longer in prison one who could do no military service.

Judge Bingham, stern man as he was, and with no warm place in his heart for a people who had brought, as he thought, such needless woe on the country, had a kindly heart, and his brave boy was dearer to him than life, and when his gentle daughter and loving wife said, "Go," he resolved to go, and he took the next train from Binghamton to Washington. He met Mr. Lincoln, stated his case, and the President did not hesitate a moment, but wrote to the Secretary of War to furnish Judge Bingham the needful authority to secure for Lieut. Roger Lawson, prisoner of war at Fort Delaware, a parole of honor of indefinite length, and to furnish him transportation to Savannah.

Roger had no idea of what was in store when the orderly came for him to report again at headquarters. As he entered the room his friend dismissed the orderly, and said: "Lieut. Lawson, let me introduce you to my father."

The old Judge stretched out his hand pleasantly, and then said, "I have something for you," and handed him the order that the Secretary of War had given him.

The poor boy was overcome, and burst into tears.

The Judge wiped his eyes as he said: "Well, I don't reckon that you are anxious to stay here any longer than you are obliged to, and as the boat starts in an hour we will go together to New York, from which place there is a transport going to start for Savannah in a very short time."

Roger pressed the hand of his noble friend, and hurried to his quarters, bade farewell to his comrades, and was soon on his way to New York. The old Judge left him at the Astor House, where he usually stopped, having paid his bill for the time that he must wait, and went back to his home in Connecticut angrier than ever with the fire eaters who had brought on the war.

Capt. Bingham had not been forgetful that Roger might need funds, and had supplied him with what was necessary.

Roger knew that a Confederate was not in high favor in New York about that time, and did not make himself prominent. He was not willing to conceal his true character, but not disposed to advertise himself. He spent in his room the two days that he was waiting for the steamer, except as he appeared in citizen's clothes at the table. He noticed a rough, gray-bearded old fellow sitting close to him and eying him very sharply. And the day before he sailed, after dinner, he was in his room when he heard a knock at his door. He went to it, and saw the old man. He came in, at Roger's invitation, and took a seat. Looking cautiously around, he said, in rather a hoarse whisper: "Look here, young man, hain't you a Confed?"

Roger smiled, and said: "Yes; I am a paroled prisoner going home from Fort Delaware."

"Well, I am Jim Anderson, once from Pike County, Missouri, but now from Santa Rosy, Californy, and did not know but that you was a tryin' to git away from 'em, and I'll be blessed if I weren't gwine to help ye."

"No; I am a paroled prisoner, and have my papers."

"Well, I've got ten gold eagles here what's been a waitin' to fly to some Confed's pocket, and these is yours."

"I thank you, and I can't refuse to take them, for I know my father was on Sherman's line, and I fear the family and the people are greatly destitute."

Well, I can't repeat what old Jim said. His

language was more emphatic than pious, but shortly he said: "Well, I mout git you into trouble, or you mout git me into trouble. Goodbye, boy, and hurrah for Jeff Davis and the Confederacy!" The old man left his new friend.

The next afternoon the steamer turned her face southward, and in three days Roger had reached Savannah.

CHAPTER XXIII.

MIDNIGHT.

GEN. LAWSON was safe from capture after Sherman had marched from Savannah, but his exposure to the chilling weather of December had brought on a severe attack of pneumonia, which had left him greatly weakened and with a fearful cough. It became evident to him and to all that his last campaign was nearing its end. He had made good preparation for that end, and the ministrations of his sweet, Christian wife and dear daughter made the evening as bright as it could be. But O for Roger! Could he but see him once more. He had no word from him for a month, and yet he could not but look toward the door as if hoping his boy would enter it. He was declining rapidly, that was evident. Wife and child and friend alike knew that the strong man was now near his end. The mind was bright, the heart was brave, but the poor body was no longer a fit tenement for the man. When Roger reached Savannah he found every railway torn up, no steamer going southward, and his only hope of reaching home was to buy a mule and to ride through the country. He was able to make the purchase without difficulty, and began his wearisome journey. He was fifty miles from home, and night was near at hand before he could begin his journey, but as soon as it was possible he started homeward. All night long he rode. The next morning he was still ten miles away from home. The mule was weary, but the rider forgot he could get weary himself. He stopped at a house long enough to give his mule some food and eat a morsel himself, and then began his journey again. He was slowly making his way over the sand beds when he heard a voice that he thought he knew, of one who was giving out a hymn and singing the words he repeated. He had often heard Jack sing. Jack was so absorbed in his song that he did not notice the stranger who had just caught sight of him until they were face to face, and Roger said: "Jack! Jack!"

"Lord, have messy! Lord, have messy! A spirit, a spirit! Mass Roger's spirit." He was too frightened to run, but he covered his eyes in terror.

"Jack, don't you know me? I am not dead. I am no spirit."

"Mass Roger, is you sure you's not dead?"

"Feel my hand and see, Jack."

"Bless de Lord! Bless de Lord! Mass Roger, you's come in time. Ole Massa is still a libbin."

"Jack, get off your mule and take mine. I must not wait."

Jack dismounted and Roger put the young mule up to his best speed. Before he reached his home, however, he realized the wisdom of preparing them for his coming, and so he restrained his eagerness and paused long enough at Mrs. John Jones's to get her to go before him.

Well, I cannot lift the veil, I cannot describe the meeting. The brave soldier as he sat in the warm sunshine of later January, looking for death with a fearless eye, now looked upon the face of him he had not hoped to see again in this world.

A week afterward a sad company surrounded the grave at the old Medway Church, where beside his ancestors Gen. Lawson was laid to sleep. He had passed over the river to rest under the shade of the trees. The night before he passed, he said: "I have lost all but my religion." As death came his mind wandered a little and he was ordering his troops in battle, and then joyously said, "We've won, we've won," and sunk to sleep.

CHAPTER XXIV.

BEGINNING ANEW.

THE almost heart-broken wife leaned upon the remaining arm of her loving boy as she walked sadly from the old graveyard where for more than a hundred years her kinspeople had been laid away. The family carriage had been left by the raiders, and in it the sad family made their way back to their pine woods home.

The troubles of life are sometimes unmixed evil, and men and women are sometimes turned to stone by them; but there are those who suffer and are blessed, for they look through every cloud and see the light, and thus did the saintly woman; and to such as she was trials are only tonics to the soul. They learn to rejoice while they weep.

Helen and Roger were young and brave, and their tender love for their mother kept them from idle lamentation. "Lawson Place" was in ashes, its chimneys as thousands of others stood as monuments of the needless cruelty of a pitiless soldier to a helpless people, and all that the family owned was swept away. Roger felt that he was now to face another foe more fearful than any he had met before. The land about him was desolate, a great social revolution was impending. He had girded himself for the conflict. Mr. Jones, whom his father had trusted so fully, and whom he had found so faithful, was still manager. Roger and Helen, however, decided that some immediate change must be made, and Mr. Jones was called into consultation. The case was a somewhat alarming one. Two hundred and fifty negroes were to be fed, and there was no corn or bacon, and but a small supply of rice, with which to feed them. Something must be done, and at once, or they would starve. To farm when there were no mules or plow horses was impossible. To attempt to make another crop where they were was folly.

Mr. Jones said: "Well, Mr. Roger and Miss Helen, its no use to say we is in a bad fix—a kind of delemmer, as Parson Prescott used to say—and we can't do nothin' but do the best we kin. So I've been a thinkin' that we had better git the hands back to 'Lawson Place' as soon as possible. Their cabins is left; them yanks never left nothin' but the graveyard and the nigger houses. The niggers all know how to make rice with a hoe, and while we can't do much for 'em, they is less likely to starve down on Medway and the salts than here. The fact is, them yanks are obleeged to feed these niggers. We can't do it. Now if you think the nigger ain't gwine to be free, you've got some property yit, but, to my seein', a nigger hain't worth more than a poor white man, and a powerful onery one at that."

"I fully agree with you, Mr. Jones, and I think we had better begin the move at once. The people may run away to the Sea Islands and the army at Savannah, but better that than starvation."

So all the slaves were sent to their old home, except a few who were left at "Pine Lodge." Mr. Jones turned them over at "Lawson Place" to their respective drivers, and returned to his home in the pine woods. Roger sent them every week from the rapidly exhausting granary what food he could, but it was evident that this could not continue long. The effort to make anything more than a small crop of provisions was abandoned, and the family was reduced to the necessity of living in the narrowest way. The parched potato gave them a substitute for coffee; rice and sweet potatoes were the breadstuff. A little bacon was scantily dealt out once or twice a week, and there was a chicken now and then, a catfish caught by old Jack in his trap, a mess of bream caught by Roger in the pond near by, and so the family was kept from real want; but there was great stringency and much privation.

At last it was all over. Gen. Lee surrendered. A few weeks afterwards Johnston followed, and then the collapse came. Roger was not surprised when it did. "Thank God!" Roger said when he heard it, "the negroes won't starve now."

"Well, maybe they will not. They freed them; now they will feed them."

Old Jack, young Jack, Aunt Judy, and Chloe only now remained on the place. The mule Roger had bought and the two mules Jack had confiscated were the stock which was left behind, and now there was coming into harvest a field of oats, which with the rice straw and pea vines, furnished sufficient forage to keep them in working order. Two bags of what is called in the South "long cotton," a variety of that which is known as "Sea Island," had escaped the torch by being hid in the swamp, and Roger with young Jack went to Savannah on the wagon to dispose of them. They brought a very large price. The two bags, weighing six hundred pounds, brought $500, which Roger received in greenbacks, but when people had been paying $30 per yard for calico and $30 a pound for coffee, to buy calico for thirty cents and bacon for twenty cents and coffee for fifty cents seemed almost cheap. He bought a cask of bacon, some flour, loaf sugar, delicious tea, and articles necessary for the ladies' apparel, and the wagon as heavily loaded as was safe returned to the place. The negroes on the plantation reported to the Freedman's Bureau, and had rations issued until they could get a crop made.

When Roger began to look into the condition of his father's affairs, he found that he was a penniless heir.

There was the Medway property, devastated and mortgaged to its full value; the "Pine Grove" property, devastated and mortgaged to its full value; the Rosevelt Factory stock, worthless; the State of Georgia Bank stock, worthless; the Atlantic and Gulf Railroad stock, worthless; fifty thousand dollars of Confederate bonds, worthless; fifty thousand dollars Confederate money for last year's crop of rice, worthless; twenty thousand dollars Georgia treasury notes, worthless. On the other hand every debt his father owed must be paid if there was means to pay it with. He had looked over the papers, and he said with rather a faint smile: "Well, my girl, we've 'Ivy Bush' left if we could get there."

"Well, why not 'Ivy Bush?'" said Helen.
"Yes, why not?"

Roger at first thought of attempting to recover what was lost. They had the plantations in possession. The negroes were there. Mr. Harris might be able to furnish the money to begin again; but if he had any such hope, it was soon dispelled by a letter from Messrs Harris & Sons. They wrote him that Messrs. Fall, Daniel & Son had written them with reference to the mortgage, that the old Quaker refused any extension of time, and that if the mortgage, principle and interest, was not paid by November 1, steps for foreclosure should at once be taken.

Roger looked a little depressed, but clear-headed Helen said: "This is best. We never could have made enough to have paid that mortgage, and we must now be content to be what God in his providence says we should be: to be poor. We will go to 'Ivy Bush.'"

"If we can get there," said her brother. "It has been three years since you heard from there at all. I don't suppose the place has run away, though."

"No; papa put old man Durham in the place when he resolved to go the war, and I suppose he is there still. But we have not been able to hear from him for three years."

"Well, we are a fixture here for the next six months, until matters are settled here, and then we will start again and live anew at 'Ivy Bush.' God has been very good to us in saving us from any suffering thus far, but when I think of how helpless I am and how little I know, and think of mamma and you, I get a little despondent."

"You worry about us. You forget, young man, I am your elder sister, and have taken pretty good care of myself in the past."

"And so you have of all the rest, but I ought not to let the load fall on you so heavily."

"When I complain, you may sympathize. If Bob had not run away with our silver and my jewels, we at least might have had something to have set us up in housekeeping."

"Well, we will be about as well off in that respect as most of our neighbors in Habersham."

The Federal soldiers were gradually withdrawn from the country, and people were adjusting themselves to the new condition of things under which they were. When the last soldier from Liberty was gone, and things had settled down to the calm repose of other days, old Jack seemed to feel greatly relieved. Roger thought maybe he was relieved because the confiscation of the two mules by young Jack had escaped discovery, but he found there was another cause. One evening after supper Jack came to the back door, and called for Roger: "Mass Roger, I want you and Miss Helen to leab ole Miss wid Judy, and come 'long wid me.

"Well, Jack, where are you going?"

"Nebber you min'; you come 'long wid me."

Young Jack was at the back door, with a spade and a mattock. The old man had a pine torch. He lit it, and led the group into the recesses of the swamp. He passed the magnolia tree under which something like a grave appeared, and muttered to himself: "Dat nigger fool one time." Striking out into the wood by an obscure path, he paused at last where there was a fallen tree of small size. He looked in several directions, then he turned to young Jack, and said: "Now you roll back dat log." He did so. "Now you dig right dar." He did so. As he dug old Jack threw the dirt aside with his spade. At last Jack's mattock struck something. "Dat's it," said the old man. The dirt was thrown out, and old Jack and his son raised out from the grave in which he had buried it the *hair-covered trunk*.

"Poor Massa never know dat rascal Bob. He truss him; I no truss him. Bob run away with de yankee man, I slip here and dig up de trunk and bury him ergin. Bob come get him; Bob no find him. I tell nobody till yankee man get gone. All de tings here, just like Massa put em." The faithful old man had been afraid to tell any human being of his secret till he knew that all danger was past.

The trunk was carried carefully home. It had not been injured, and the contents were not at all affected. In it was the family silver: urn, coffee-pot, teapot, cups, spoons, the old watches, and diamonds. It was old time silver, when silverware was known as plate, and when over a hundred dollars was often paid for a cup richly chased, or a tea urn. There too was the deed made to " Ivy Bush," and the will of Roger Lawson.

It was impossible to get to " Ivy Bush " during the summer of 1865, and Roger remained at home, settling up his father's affairs as best he could. A letter to Durham failed to elicit any reply, and Roger wrote to his old friend, Squire Bass, of whom he had not heard in four years. It took a letter a long time to get to Clarksville, for the mail service was but slowly restored, and it was toward winter when he received this astounding reply:

NEAR CLARKSVILLE, Dec. 1, 1865.

My Dear Roger: I was glad to hear from you. The Lord has been mighty good to me and my old woman and Jeems, and we is all back agin. Jeems was wounded pretty bad in the fight before Knoxville, but he's pretty nigh over it, though his leg troubles him yit. You writ about "Ivy Bush." Well, I am sorry to say old Bob Durham is thar yit, and he says he's a gwine to stay thar. He says what I know's a lie: that he bought the place from your pappy, and is got a deed. He's got a deed, for I seed it; and it was signed by your pappy, he says. Well, its got his name to it, and it looks like he writ it; but I don't think he did. The last time he was here he told me he had give this place to your mother, and I know he wern't the man to go back on his word. I am afeerd old Bob is a gwine to give you trouble, but you can count on me and Jeems a standing by you. The Durham boys deserted the army, and jined the bushwhackers in Tennessee. They are back here now, and the country hain't no better for their being in it. Old Bob Durham drinks a power, and the boys is no doubt making blockade whisky, but the revenues don't try to catch up with 'em. I think you had better come up here as soon as you kin git here. The longer this thing is put off the more trouble thar will be. We have had hard times up here, and they is hard yit. The boys didn't git back in time to pitch a good crap, but, thank God, we haven't starved, and we hain't a gwine to. Give a heap of howdy to Helen and your mother from me and my old woman and Jeems.

Your true friend, JAMES BASS.

Roger read the letter with mingled feelings of astonishment and indignation. It was evident that, taking advantage of the war times and the long distance which separated the parties, and hoping that death would assist them in their schemes, a plot had been entered into to rob them of their summer place. Roger knew enough of the slow processes of law and of its uncertainties not to feel concerned. He handed the letter silently to Helen. When she read it her cheek flushed; but, looking at her brother and seeing the evidences of great anxiety in his face, she calmly said: "God still lives, and he will not allow this robbery. We will find some way out of this trouble too."

"I know that we will, but I am annoyed at the distress that it will give poor mamma."

"Why need she to know anything of it? We can keep it to ourselves."

"Yes, and we will do so. It is evident that nothing can be done now. It is difficult to get to Habersham. I cannot leave mother. There is little hope of doing anything on the farm if we could get possession of it this season. So will let the matter rest till summer."

The two children went out unto the room of their mother. Never demonstrative, but always tender and thoughtful, she was thinking for others. When they came they found that she had opened the trunk and had placed on the table the articles that it contained. There were one teapot, one coffee urn, one punch bowl, one salver, one sugar bowl, twelve large tablespoons, twelve dessert spoons, twelve teaspoons, one soup tureen and ladle, one large pitcher, one flagon, one-half dozen goblets, and sundry other pieces of heavy solid silver. These pieces of silver had descended from the Maxwells and Lawsons, and had the court of arms of each family on them. There was a diamond brooch, a pair of diamond bracelets, a pearl necklace, and some beautiful rings set with diamonds, sapphires, and pearls. As the children came in she said to them: " I am taking a little list of these things, and a last look at them. After your dear father's death I determined to have the plate on my table no more, and now that my children need the money which it will sell for, I am anxious for it to be sold."

The children were at first disposed to demur, but it was too evidently the thing that ought to be done for them to hesitate, and so it was decided that Roger should take it to Mr. Hamilton, the Savannah jeweler, and place it in his hands to be disposed of. Helen insisted that her jewels should be sold too.

CHAPTER XXV.

SOME UNLOOKED-FOR EVENTS.

THE next day Roger, with young Jack and the wagon in which was the trunk of plate, began his journey to Savannah, which he reached in due time. The war was virtually over; but the country was still under military rule, and the cities in charge of provost marshals. To see the colored troops in blue uniform parading the streets of Savannah, and to be forced to submit his papers to their examination, was not a pleasant thing to a high-spirited young Southerner like Roger, and when to all this was added the fact of a lost cause and lost fortunes, and above all of a lost father, the cup was sufficiently full of bitterness.

Roger had little now to do than to deposit the plate with his mother's old jeweler, and to request him to do the best that he could with it, and to call on Col. Floyd, who was his father's counselor at law, and consult him about the "Ivy Bush" matter. He called at the office of the wise attorney, and told him the condition of affairs at "Ivy Bush." Roger showed him Squire Bass's letter, and when the Colonel read it he looked thoughtful: " Well, Captain, I am sure that your case is a good one, and in time you can oust these intruders, but the times are out of joint. The courts are not in good working order, and it is certain that you cannot trust a jury now. Old Durham has evidently quite a following. He seems to be a Unionist. His sons were in the Federal army, and he has a deed; forged as it is, it is a deed, and has been admitted to record, and the best thing that you can do is to do nothing now. Write to Col. Billups, who was in the army with your father and is a good lawyer, to keep an eye on old Durham, and see to it that no sale of the place is made to an innocent purchaser, and wait for developments."

This was in accord with Roger's own ideas of what was best, and so he went back to the home in Liberty to wait. He carried with him from the colonel's office sundry law books which he intended to study under his direction, that he might get ready for admission to the bar.

In the *Savannah Press* of May 31 appeared this advertisement:

FAMILY PLATE AT A SACRIFICE.

A planter's wife who has lost her property, and who has been bereft of her husband, offers a beautiful lot of silverware and some beautiful old time jewelry for sale at a great sacrifice. Apply to Hamilton & Co., 41 Broughton Street.

A Federal colonel was smoking in the office of the commandant, and a young adjutant was reading the morning paper. The advertisement caught his eye. "Hey, colonel! here is something the bummers did not get. Pride has its fall. I see these haughty dames, who toss their pretty heads at us, have to come down at last," and he read the advertisement. "Say, colonel, let us go down and look at it, and if it is cheap I believe I'll get it for my girl in Maine."

The colonel did not seem to enter into the spirit of the thoughtless subordinate, but quietly arose and said: "Well, come on."

Mr. Hamilton brought out the plate. "There are," he said, "two crests here—the Maxwells and the Lawsons. They were of our oldest and best families in Liberty County, but Gen. Lawson was wounded and died and the old home was burned down, and his wife was forced to sell. The plate is of the highest grade of crown silver."

"The Maxwells and Lawsons, of Liberty County, did you say?"

"Yes."

"Was this lady the mother of Capt. Roger Lawson?"

"Yes. He put the plate in my hands."

"What is it worth?"

"Well, I ought to get $1,000 for the lot; and for these jewels I got when I sold them to her father $500 more. I might take less, as they are in such need, but they are richly worth that."

"Mr. Jeweler," said the adjutant, "say $500 for the lot."

"No; I will try to do better than that."

"Well, I'll give that, but no more."

They went quietly out of the store, but in an hour's time an orderly came back to the store with this note:

Dear Sir: Inclosed find check for $1,500 in full payment of the plate and jewelry shown me this morning. Send the goods by the bearer.

The next mail to "Pine Lodge" brought Roger and Helen a surprising letter.

Capt. Roger Lawson.

My Dear Sir: The day after you left the plate in my charge a young yankee colonel came in and bought the whole of it. He had it sent to his office. His name I do not know. The money is to your credit in the Central Railroad Bank.

HAMILTON & Co.

CHAPTER XXVI.

HOW BOB DURHAM LOST HIS CASE.

THE times were truly out of joint. There was first the government of Georgia as it has been for a hundred years, but it only stood a few months. Then the provisional government, and then the military government. They came in such rapid succession that one was scarcely able to locate the government before it was gone. There was a breaking up of everything, and in no part of Georgia were things more mixed than in that part of the State which bordered on North Carolina and Tennessee. Here alone, as far as Georgia was concerned, it was that the loyalist element had much influence, but here it did. Some lawyers of real parts were avowed radicals, and many of the people.

Col. McNiel was one of the leaders of what the old Confederates scornfully called "Hogbacks." He was hand in glove with the moonshiners, who were themselves on the best of terms with the revenue men. The Colonel had drawn up, he said, the deed to "Ivy Bush" by which Bob Durham held it. Col. Billups knew all these people, and was on as good terms with them as a Confederate colonel could be with Union men. Some he knew were honest, but some he knew were thoroughly unscrupulous. He was too wise to act precipitately, so he advised Roger to remain quietly at "Pine Lodge" until he sent for him, and kept his eyes wide open. At length, in March of 1866, he wrote Roger to come on to Clarksville as soon as possible. The court was near its spring term. Old Bob Durham had decided to sell out, and was about to trade with a man from over the line in Tennessee. Issue must be made at once, and Roger must be there to secure possession, if possession could be secured.

When Roger reached Clarksville he found the Basses ready to welcome him, and his old friend, Andy Rhodes, was back in his old haunts. They had been in the army together. When Andy was seriously sick in the mountains Roger had nursed him as tenderly as a brother. Andy had an eighth part of Indian blood in his veins. He feared nothing but work. He was the only man in Habersham the Durhams were really afraid of, and it was a rather good thing for Roger that Andy was his friend.

When Roger reached Clarksville he had an interview with Col. Billups.

Matters were a little squally. Old Durham had the deed, McNiel drew it up, the witnesses were dead, Durham was about to sell, and he and his sons swore vengeance against any man who disturbed their right of possession. It would never do to have the matter before a jury, with McNiel to persuade it and the Durhams to frighten it. He must try another course. Roger was to be quiet, and simply wait.

"Say, Billups," said McNiel, "it is a poor business to molest that poor old man, Durham. I drew the deed myself, and old Bob paid his hard-earned money for the land. He has held it for four years, and it's too late for this youngster to pretend the property was given to his mother. You had just as well let it drop."

"Well, Dick, maybe you are right. Anyway, you get the deed and bring it to my office, where I will meet you; and bring old Bob there, and I will get my young client, and we will see if we can't settle it."

So old Bob and Col. McNiel and Col. Billups and Roger met in the office, and with them came Andy Rhodes. Col. Billups told him he must be on hand, and ready for work, if work was needed. Andy knew what that meant, and as he buckled on his cavalry belt he looked a little carefully at the cartridges in his navy shooter, and put on some fresh caps.

The little group were evidently intensely in earnest.

"Now, Col. Billups, I drew this deed; didn't I, Bob?"

"Yes, that you did, Squire, and Bob Wortham and Tom Hughes both witnessed it. It was just before Maj. Lawson left here for the army. He come up here to fix things, and carry his niggers back, and says he: 'Mr. Durham,' says he, 'I need some money, and I don't think I'll ever come back here no more, and I'll sell you this 'ere place for $800 cash down.' That's just what the deed says, ain't it, Squire? And says I, 'I'll take it.' And, Squire, you drawed the deed and seed me pay down the money, didn't you?"

"Yes, of course I did."

"And now for em to bring another deed, what they say was made a year before this un, and try to git my propity from me, hain't honest, and I hain't a gwine to put up with it nuther. Thar'll be some blood spilt first."

"O well, Bob!" said Col. Billups quietly, "nobody is going to spill any blood about it. If your deed is good, it is good. On the court records, though, there is a deed which was made a year before this was, in favor of Mrs. Mary Lawson."

"Yes, I know thar was, but I did not know it when I bought this property, and you didn't; did you, Squire?"

"No, of course I did not. I did not think a rich man like Col. Lawson would rob a poor countryman out of his honest earnings."

"What do you mean, sir?" said Roger, starting to his feet, and clinching his fist.

"Please be still, Mr. Lawson," said Col. Billups. "Suppose, Dick, somebody forged a deed, and signed Lawson's name to it." Col. Billups had the deed in his hand, and looked calmly in McNiel's eye.

"Somebody forged! Do you dare to say I forged it?" he hissed as he rose to his feet and reached for his pistol.

"Say, Dick McNiel, you just sit there quiet, will ye, and listen to Col. Billups, or I'll put five bullets into ye so quick you won't have time to wink." The navy of Andy never missed fire, and he never missed his mark. Old Bob had started up, too, with his pistol in his hand, but Roger's pistol warned him to be still, and he dropped his weapon and sunk into his seat.

"Yes, Dick, you forged that deed, and it is not

the first by many, I am afraid. But you were not as sharp as you thought you were. Your pretended witnesses are dead, that is true; the record was made, that is true; your deed is dated 1861, that is true; but, Dick, you did not get the right kind of paper, if you did stain it. Look here." And he held the deed up to the light, and in the body of it one read: "Passaic Mills, 1865." The telltale figures settled the case. The lawyer, cowed and pale, said nothing.

"Now, Dick, if this case comes before Judge Knight, you'll go to the penitentiary; but for your wife's sake it shan't go there. But you must go away from Clarksville, and stay away, and if so I'll keep the secret. And now, Bob Durham, you old villain, if you are not out of "Ivy Bush" by to-morrow night you and Dick McNiel both will be indicted for conspiracy and forgery and perjury."

"Well, Colonel, I was a gwine to leave anyhow. Col. McNiel told me to do just what I did. I didn't mean no harm."

And so "Ivy Bush" came back to its owners.

CHAPTER XXVII.

AT THE BOTTOM OF THE LADDER.

COL. BILLUPS had become much interested in his young friend. The father of Roger had been his brigade commander in Virginia, and there was a warm affection between the two officers; and when Roger asked what he was to pay for his services, the Colonel refused to receive any compensation. After Roger had told him of the loss of everything, and of his anxiety to be admitted to the bar, the Colonel said to him: "Well, apply now. You have read enough law to begin to practice, and I am sure you can pass an approved examination. And as you are going to move to this county, it is best for you to be admitted in this court."

So Roger made his application, and was examined by a committee of lawyers. After it was over Judge Knight said to him: "Your examination, Mr. Lawson, has been very creditable. You show an unusual acquaintance with the principles of law, and are well up in your reading. I predict for you a bright future."

The next thing to be done was to remove the family, so Roger went to Liberty. He found his father's old manager not unwilling to take "Pine Lodge" in full payment for all arrears.

"The fact is, Mr. Roger," said the overseer, "I mout have managed niggers, and I reckon I did, pretty well when they was niggers; but now, when a nigger is a little better than a white man, somebody else can git my job. I am a gwine to stay in the pine woods and git along without 'em."

There were few debts to pay, and the devastation of Sherman's army had made it an easy matter to move what they left behind them. Old Jack and Aunt Judy, and young Jack and Chloe, and Mammy were going to move with the family. "The truth is, Missus," said Mammy, "I's been takin' car' of you so long I's just obleeged to go wid you."

There were the three mules and the wagon, and Roger traded off some cows which had escaped the raiders, and bought another mule. They had the carriage still, and the wagon, and the lighter goods were loaded in the wagon, and the heavier goods sold; and in their own conveyances they made the slow journey toward their new old home. There was still several hundred dollars of the money for which the plate was sold, but there was quite a family of helpless dependents to be provided for. Old Jack and Mammie had done no hard work for years, Aunt Judy had done nothing but cook, and Chloe was simply a housemaid. The young readers of this chronicle have read but little if they have not seen many allusions to the fate of the poor negroes, who gave two hundred years of unrequited labor to their white masters. The fact was, no race of mere laborers were ever better paid, for no race was ever so universally provided for as this race was. The able-bodied were by no means all who were to be fed and clothed, and the consumers were always greatly more numerous than the producers. To Roger, to abandon these faithful old slaves was not to be thought of, and so Mammy had her place in the carriage and old Jack on the driver's seat, as he had done in all the years gone by. Old Squire Bass had insisted that the family should be brought at once to his home, and should remain there until the effects of Bob Durham's shiftless ways could be remedied. The warm greeting of the motherly old woman was all the more tender because of the sad changes which had passed over the home of her friend.

The prospect before the brave young soldier was not a bright one: A farm, neglected and run down; a house, dilapidated, with no furniture in it; three helpless old negroes, and an invalid mother and delicate sister; a profession just entered upon, and all the way untried, was before him. His heart grew somewhat faint at the prospect, but he could not forget how God had blessed them in the past, and he could trust him for the future. As they passed through Athens he had purchased some plain furniture and some needful supplies, for which he was to send the wagon after the travelers had reached their destination. While they were waiting for these things, and while the servants were getting the house in habitable shape, the little family remained at the home of Squire Bass.

Up to this time they had not realized how changed was their worldly condition, and now as Roger saw himself a poor, dependent, and helpless man, while he cared little for himself, he could not but feel great anxiety for his mother and Helen. Upon them as yet no real hardship had come, but what was now before them?

There were no people who faced the great changes after the war with a braver heart than many of those who had been brought up in luxury, and on none did the storm blow with a fiercer blast. Roger and Helen were not braver than ten thousand others who found themselves paupers when they had been princes, and Roger might have despaired but for his sister's courage and his mother's faith. Helen was never so bright and cheery. The poor mother was too sad at the remembrance of what had been to consider the outside surroundings. The only seriously discontented one was Aunt Judy. She took her vengeance out on Chloe, whom she scolded unmercifully, and found some relief in the bitterness with which she denounced "dem poor trash w'at's bin tryin' to tief Master's place."

The wagon, with the plain poplar bedsteads, the cheap washstand and bureau, had arrived, and then it was sent over to Squire Bass's after the bedding, which had been left there. Throwing her palmetto hat on her curls, Helen coiled herself up on the mattresses and rode over to "Ivy Bush" as joyously as a schoolgirl.

"Bless her dear heart," said the old lady, "she is just as happy as if she had not lost her fortune."

When the mother came "Ivy Bush" was like home again. The hardships of war had been good discipline for people who were to lose all, and "Pine Lodge" had prepared the way for "Ivy Bush." Aunt Judy had seen to it that the house was neatly scoured, and Helen had made her mother's chamber as cosy as a daughter's good good taste could make it. The honeysuckle and sweet shrub sent their fragrance through the chamber, a nice supper had been prepared, and when James Bass brought over the mother in the afternoon "Ivy Bush" looked like home again.

CHAPTER XXVIII.

ROGER LAWSON, ATTORNEY AT LAW.

THE next day after the family were snugly housed was Sunday. It was the day when the circuit preacher came to his appointment. The good mother was not strong enough to go out to service, but Roger and Helen went, and Roger put his Church certificate into the preacher's hand and announced himself as ready for work. The Sunday school had not been organized for want of a superintendent, and the preacher in charge selected the young lawyer for the place. The people around the church were many of them very ignorant, as they were very poor, and Helen and Roger found a large field for any work they wished to do, and I have always found it to be a fact that if we are willing to do the work nearest to us we always find enough of it.

Col. Billups had kindly invited Roger to share his office, and gave him the use of his books, and proffered to give him such instruction as an old lawyer could give to a young one. "Now, Lawson," he said, "you have just begun to prepare for work. You know enough law to begin to practice, and enough to begin the careful study. You are here in a quiet, retired country town, and it is little likely there will ever be a demand for a knowledge of those subjects which have engaged the best legal minds, but my idea is that the briefless lawyer of a country village should fit himself to be the Chief Justice of the United States. I have here a library which, while not large, has the best books in it. Some of these came from my father; many of them I have bought for myself. I have studied questions concerning trusts, remainders, tenures, inheritances which I have never met with, and never expected to meet with, but when I do meet with them I am ready for them. Another thing, when you have a case do not consider the amount of the fee nor the importance of the case. Prepare as carefully for a case before Squire Larkins as for one before the Supreme Court. I am not going to take you into partnership, not because I am not willing to divide practice with you, but because it will be best for you to win your own spurs. If you were to win a case by your labor alone, and were my partner, I would get the credit for it; but all I can do for you I will do. My office is yours and my books are yours, so put up your shingle and go to work."

The young lawyer learns very soon that he must be patient, that there is no easy way to success, and while Roger did not enjoy his want of practice, he obeyed the Colonel's counsel, and gave himself to hard study.

Old Jack took charge of the farm. He could not work much, but he could superintend.

Young Jack, had married Chloe, and taken her to a cabin of her own, where Aunt Judy could no longer reproach her for her divers shortcomings. Young Jack was the only active worker, and as it was not likely that the farm would do much more than pay its own way, and as the deposit in the Central Railroad Bank was getting alarmingly low, the question of fees became one of real importance.

At last Roger got a case, if not a fee. The poor woman who came to his office was a forlorn specimen of that class of people known all over the South by different names: sometimes as "crackers," sometimes as "mossbacks," sometimes as "sand lappers," and sometimes as "poor whites." They were born in poverty and brought up in ignorance. They had always lived in log cabins, and always on hard fare. They were, many of them, pure, honest, kind-hearted, and in their way religious. They were often land owners, and not unfrequently rose from their lowly estate into a higher place. James Jenkins was a good specimen of this class. He had moved over from Anderson, in South Carolina, to Habersham some years before, and settled on a little farm on Duke's Creek. The farm had only forty acres in it, and of these only twenty were free from timber; but it was productive, and the plain man lived a contented and an independent life upon it. The war broke out, and he left the farm to go into the army. He took his young wife and her four children to her father's, in South Carolina. He rented the farm, but the party renting it had gone away and left it.

Bill Hillborn was a land stealer, and when he saw that the place was vacated he took possession of it, and claimed it as his own.

Jenkins went with McMillan's regiment to the war, and there was no braver man or better soldier in Lee's army; but when Gettysburg was fought, and the shattered Twenty-fourth came off the field, Jenkins was missing. His comrades never knew what became of him. He was abreast with the foremost in that awful charge when they saw him last. In a grave marked "unknown" he sleeps on Pennsylvania soil. He never knew why there was a war. Indeed, he hardly knew that there was a North. He merely knew, he said, that "Bob McMillan was raisin' a rigiment, and that he ought to fight for libbuty, as his granddaddy had done in the Revolution war."

Poor Nancy Jenkins, with her four children, was on her father's little farm in Anderson, S. C., when her husband was killed. The war had been two years over when her father died, and she was homeless. She got a kind neighbor to bring her over the mountains to her old home in Georgia. When she reached it she found a stranger in the cabin. He had rented it, he said, from Squire Hillborn, and had put in his crops, and while he was mighty sorry for the poor woman, he could not help her. She could stay here until she could get some satisfaction, he said, and that he would go with her to Clarksville to see a lawyer about her rights.

She came to see Col. Billups, and told him her story. He had known her husband, and he believed her story, but he told her at once that he was the attorney for Hillborn in several important cases, and could not take the case, but introduced her to Roger. "You see," she said to the young attorney, "when me and Jim was married my pappy give me a hundred dollars, and Jim had made another hundred, and as he had a critter and a little waggin and I had some things, we thought that we'd strike out for ourselves. So weuns come over here, and Mr. Richardson, what is gone somewhar, I don't know whar, but I heerd it was to the Alabam, he sold Jim a little plantation up on the crick. Thar warn't a stick amiss on it when we bought it, but we went up thar and built our cabin, and was gittin' on right peart when this here awful war come on, and he went to the army, and that is the last I ever seed of him. I couldn't write, and I couldn't git back till arter daddy died, and then I had nowhar to go. I got Mr. Smith to bring me here, and when I got back I found that Bill Hillborn said that he'd bought our plantation, and I jist know that he didn't, and I want you to take the law on him, and git it back for me and my children."

"Well, Mrs. Jenkins," said Roger, "where is your deed?"

"The deed? What's that?"

"Why, the paper Mr. Richardson gave your husband."

"Why no! I never seed that arter Jim left with Mr. Richardson to go to the Squire's, but I know it's my land."

"Do you know whether the deed was recorded?"

"Why, I don't know what you mean by accorded!"

"Recorded! I mean, did he give it to the clerk?"

"I don't know. There was two or three clerks in Mr. Stanford's store, where we use to trade, and he mout a given it to one of 'em; but I know it's my lan'."

"Well, I am sure it is. Now you go back there *and stay.* I think Mr. Moore will let you stay on the place, and I will do my best for you. Who was the squire to whom your husband went when he bought the land?"

"Why, Squire Williams, in Nacoochee."

"Is he there now?"

"No; he's gone too."

"Do you know where?"

"No; I hain't hearn."

"Well, I will do all I can for you, but I can't promise much; but you try and stay on the land."

The first thing to do was to see Hillborn. This land trader was famous for his large holding of wild lands. He succeeded in getting tract after tract, and it was rumored that his papers were often none of the best. He was always in court, and often victorious, seldom defeated. He was oily and plausible, and had money. Roger called him into his office, and asked him about the land.

"Well, Squire," said Hillborn, "the poor woman thinks she's got a right. Jim did live on the place, but I let him live thar for nothin', for I believe in bein' good to pore folks, and I never charged nothin'; but I have a deed from Billy Richardson to Dick McNiel, and I bought it from him, and the deed's done recorded. I'm sorry for her, but I can't help her. I'm a pore man myself, and you know the Scriptur' says: 'He that provideth not for his own house is wus than a infidel.'"

There seemed but little hope for the widow. The deed from Richardson seemed all right, and Richardson was gone, the squire who witnessed it was gone, and the other witnesses were gone; and yet Roger was sure she spoke truly. He must use a little strategy.

Dick Moore, who was tenant, had a kind heart, and Bill Hillborn was a hard landlord. Dick was sure the widow had a just claim, and so he agreed with Roger to quietly vacate the house before his time was out, and leave the widow in possession. Then the suit of ejectment must come from Hillborn.

Hillborn did not live in Habersham, but in Cherokee, and it was only after Moore was out of the way and the widow was in her cabin that he found out the true *status*. He was in a towering rage. He came to the cabin, dismounting at the gate. "Hello!" he said, for he saw a large cur dog on the front steps, and was afraid to come in. "Who lives here?"

"The owners of this place, that's who!" said a determined voice.

"I am the owner of this place."

"No; that you hain't!"

"Well, I will show you that I am! so you'd better leave here."

"But I hain't a gwine to do it!"

"Well, I'll put you out," and he started as though he would come in.

"You will? Well, I reckon you won't!" and she reached over the door and brought down her husband's single-barrel shotgun. "This gun's loaded with buckshot, Bill Hillborn, and if ye step in that gate I'll put the whole load in ye. Say, Tige, watch him!"

The cur bristled and showed his teeth.

Muttering "I'll take the law on ye," the discomfited land stealer went his way to Cleveland, to see a lawyer and get ready for the suit of ejectment.

Possession was nine-tenths of the law, but not ten-tenths. The widow was not likely to be ejected by a justice of the peace, but when the court came on, if Richardson could not be found, the deed might stand.

Roger's old friend, Squire Bass, might help him to find Richardson. He mentioned it to him.

"Why yes, Roger; I know jist whar he is. He sold out here, and went over to Randolph County, in the Alabam. I got a letter from him a little while ago. His post office is Wedowee."

"Do you think I can get him here to court?"

"Why, yes. When he writ me last winter he said he would be here after craps was laid by, if he could come; and I expect he'll be glad to come."

The court came on. There was but little business in Cleveland, and the judge called the case of " Richard Roe for Wm. Hillborn *vs.* John Doe and Mary Jenkins, writ of ejectment." Col. Billups having refused to take the case, Billy Martin, a young lawyer, was employed by Hillborn. The young lawyer said the case was a plain one. The property was his client's, and the deed produced would show the chain of deeds to Hillborn from Richardson and McNiel. The poor woman was doubtless demented. The terrible war, which the gentlemen of the jury knew was a rich man's war and a poor man's fight, had unsettled her mind. He would make no speech, but just introduce the two deeds as witnesses. He presented the deeds. 1. A deed from Billy Richardson to Richard McNiel. 2. A deed from McNiel to Hillborn. He had no other witness to present. "And now," he said, "the case is with you, my Brother Lawson."

"Mr. Sheriff," said Lawson, "call Billy Richardson."

"Billy Richardson! Billy Richardson! Billy Richardson! Come into court!"

William Hillborn turned pale, and paler still when in walked Billy Richardson, who sold him the land.

Roger, after he had sworn the witness, asked him: "What is your name?"

"Billy Richardson."

"Where do you live?"

"In Alabama."

"Did you ever live in this county?"

"I did."

"Did you get a patent to lot No. 205, Fifth District of Habersham?"

"I did."

"Did you sell that land to Dick McNiel?"

"I did not."

"Did you ever sell it?"

"I did."

"To whom?"

"To James Jenkins."

"Did you sign this deed?"

"I did not."

The lawyer for Hillborn got up and said: "May it please the Court, I beg to withdraw from this case at this juncture. The deed upon which I based my plea is undoubtedly a forgery. Whether with cognizance of my client or without it, I cannot tell. I hope your Honor will order a verdict for the defendant."

"The court," said the judge, "orders a verdict for the defendant, with all costs to the plaintiff."

The grateful woman burst into tears as she turned to Roger. "God bless you, Squire," she said; "if the pra'rs of a widow 'oman will do you any good, you shall have 'em, but that's all I've got to pay."

Hillborn came to Roger as soon as court adjourned. "Well, Colonel, I'll take my affidavy I paid good money to Dick McNiel for that land, and I was a gwine to let the widder stay thar. I just wanted my rights."

"Well, Squire," said Roger, "you will save yourself another suit and some trouble, some hard questions, if you pay this widow the back rent for the six years you've had the land, for I will prosecute you on the criminal side and sue you on the civil side of the court if you do not settle at once."

"Well, Colonel, that's pretty hard, but a man must put up with a heap of wrong things in this wicked world, even if he is honest. I don't know much, and Dick McNiel was a smart lawyer, and he cheated me; but I am willing to do something for the widder. I never got nothin' from the place scacely, but I'll pay her $25 and drop it."

"No, Squire, you can't get off that easy. If you will give the widow a good horse and forty bushels of corn which Moore owed you for rent and all the fodder and $25 in money, I'll drop the case; but if you don't, I'll have you arrested to-night for a conspiracy to defraud, and have the grand jury to take your case in hand."

"Well, Squire, I ain't the man to contend. I'd ruther folks would wrong me than wrong them, so I'll do it."

The papers were fixed, and the poor widow went to her home with a happy heart.

Roger's skill in managing the case excited much admiration, and his noble devotion to the penniless woman placed him in a high place in the hearts of the people of both counties; but there were no fees, and the deposit in Savannah was about gone. But acts like this of Roger are not apt to escape the notice of a good Lord, and he knows how to bring us out of the most trying embarrassments. So our young lawyer found it. The section in which he had his home bordered on the gold fields of Upper Georgia. Indeed, the first gold ever discovered in Georgia was discovered in Habersham County in 1829. An English company had invested largely in the mines, and it was now having a long canal dug through the county. There was much legal work to be done, and Mr. Sterling, who was the manager of the company, was looking for a solicitor. He was in the courthouse when Roger won his first case. He was so pleased with the young attorney that he decided to try and secure him for a solicitor for the company, and to Roger's astonishment and gratification he offered him one hundred dollars per month as salary, and paid the first month down in advance.

With a heart full of gratitude to God the young lawyer returned home to bear the good tidings to Helen and his mother. The question of his future was now pretty well settled. He won his way rapidly, and before he had been at the bar twelve months he had won an independent position as a lawyer. He was enabled now to provide greater comforts for his mother and sister and lay the foundation for the library he so much needed. It was well for him that he had a preceptor so wise as Col. Billups, and that he followed so faithfully his counsel. He had not completed his education even so far as the schools could carry him, and his reading for his profession had been largely devoted to the books bearing upon the practice; but now he enlarged his area of study, and made himself acquainted with those liberal studies which lie at the foundation of all true culture. He little knew how soon his knowledge of the history of the past should stand him in good place in an important position.

CHAPTER XXIX.

A DARK CHAPTER IN AMERICAN HISTORY.

TO write the story of Roger I must needs say something of the political condition of the country just after the war, but I assure my readers that if I could justly do so I would never refer to the events recorded in this chapter. The courage with which the North fought for the Union; the brave effort of the South to save the Constitution, as she read it, were events worthy of all admiration, and both participants could be commended; but how any American who was freeborn, and who held to the traditions of the past, could believe that the reconstruction measures adopted after the war was over were defensible, save as measures born of times when men were in no condition to think coolly or act justly, I cannot see. This is not the place to tell the story of how Gov. Jenkins was deposed, and how Gov. Johnson was placed in office, and of how Gen. Ruger, a general in the army, superseded him; of how the negroes were given the right of franchise, and a convention to reorganize everything was called, and of how the old and wise men of the country were shut out from places in that convention. The civilization of our section was fearfully menaced. Men a thousand miles away, utterly ignorant of the difficulties in the way and ruled by bitter partisanship, were forcing upon their countrymen measures which threatened the very destruction of all social life.

The men who were thus experimenting were sufficiently honest, and as far as they knew were acting wisely, but the certain ruin which would have resulted if their measures had been carried out would not have been less ruin because the parties who wrought it meant no ill.

There were four classes of white people who were concerned and formed parties. There was a large majority of the people who held on to most of the old traditions. They were willing to surrender those, and those only, which the fortunes of war had forced them to give up. Two things, slaveholding and the right to nullify and secede, were among the things surrendered. They were willing to recognize the civil right of the negro before the law as equal to their own, but they were not willing to show him any special favor nor invest him with political power. The Southern Republicans were willing to go farther than their conservative fellow-citizens, and accept as wisest what the moderate Republicans said must be done, negro suffrage and all, and to give what they claimed. Then there were the scalawags, renegade Southerners, who were willing to do anything to secure place and money; and then there were the carpetbaggers, adventurous Northerners, who saw an opportunity to secure positions of honor in the South which their obscurity forbade their hoping to secure in the land from which they came.

It was evident to thoughtful men that the wisest and truest were needed as they were never needed before, but by the strange infatuation which marked the times they were forbidden to take part in the convention.

To the promising young men who had not been excluded the country turned with hope, and when the election came Roger Lawson was chosen a delegate from his county. I am not writing history, nor even giving facts which can be established by the records, so the readers of the account of the Georgia Convention will look in vain for the name of Roger Lawson, as one might search for that of Bois Gilbert among the ancient Crusaders or Rob Roy in Scottish annals. Perhaps those who read between the lines may meet no difficulty in finding the place our young soldier took in the celebrated convention.

The Georgia Republicans and the more moderate carpetbaggers joined with the young men to prevent the absolute ruin of the State.

Among the members of the Convention was another Lawson, Robert Lawson, from Liberty. He was very black, but no member of the convention was in more perfect form. His dress was faultless, his manners were perfect, for no man understood the usage of good society better than our old friend, Bob. He had gone with the Federals, and had been employed as body servant by one of the generals. He went with his new master to Massachusetts, and was there treated with distinguished courtesy. He took on the manners of the people among whom he was, and when he came back to Liberty he felt that he was ready to take any position of dignity and trust. He joined the Loyal League, he was selected as their standard bearer, and he was elected to the convention. He was well dressed, well behaved, and silent, and so made a good average member. He generally watched the course of the leading Radicals, and took that. When Roger met him the former master was as kind as he used to be when Bob waited on the table, and while Bob called him Colonel instead of Mass Roger, he had evidently still a warm place in his heart for his former owner. They were equals now before the law, and in many places Robert Lawson, the colored gentleman from Liberty, was in higher esteem than the independent young rebel from Habersham.

The times were perilous. The carpetbaggers were shrewd, ambitious, and unscrupulous; the scalawags, subservient and venial; the Georgia Republicans, cautious; and the young Democrats, daring and defiant. A measure came before the convention that was very menacing. The making of the provision would bring about very serious results. The carpetbaggers were, to a man, in favor of it, as were the scalawags. The moderate Republicans opposed it, and so did the Democrats, and it depended upon the negro vote how it would go, and the negro contingent was largely led by the "gentleman from Liberty," as the President of the Convention called him.

Judge Bone, Republican, one of the leaders of the moderates, came to Roger, who led the young Democrats: "Lawson, if these fellows have their way, the State is ruined; and they will have it, unless you can do some mighty fine work with the niggers. Your old servant, Bob, is the leader among them. If you can get him to oppose the bill, you can save the State. It is worth trying. I have done my best with him; but Azariah

Fuller, from Maine, has a stronger hold on him than a Southern man. If you can't control him, the case is hopeless."

As Roger passed Bob at adjournment he said to him: " Bob, come to my room at the National to-night. I want to see you."

" Tank you, Colonel. I'll present myself dar, sah, on de proper time."

When he came in and Roger had given him a chair and a cigar, he said to him: " Well, Bob, times have changed, haven't they?"

" Yes, Mass Colonel; times is changed."

" But, Bob, you are a Georgian?"

" Yes, sah."

"And a Liberty County man?"

" Yes, sah."

" From the old Medway neighborhood?"

" Dat's a fac'."

" They were a great people?"

" Dat dey was, Mass Colonel."

" Bob, you've got their reputation in your keeping."

" Surely, sah "—

" Bob, will you disgrace them?"

" No, sah."

" Bob, will you be led around like a slave by any white man?"

" No, sah. I's free. I's gwine to stay free."

"Now, Bob, will you let Mr. Azariah Fuller lead you by the nose?"

"No, sah, not if I knows myself."

"Well, Bob, that's what he thinks he will do, and that's what I think he is not going to do. Now, Bob, when that vote comes to-morrow, show yourself a Liberty County gentleman, and act the man. Just get up and say: 'Mr. President, I've nothing against my old owners, sir, and I want peace, and I am a going to vote against that bill.' Don't say anything to Fuller; keep quiet. Bob, did I ever go back on you?"

"Never, Mass Roger, nebber no time."

"Well, you can count on me now, and I'll count on you."

The people held their breath when the ayes and nays were called the next day, and when the name of Mr. Lawson, of Liberty, was called, Bob rose. He was dressed, as usual, in the height of style. He had the air of a statesman. In a stentorian voice he said: "Mr. Prisident, sir, I's nuthin' agin my old owners, sah; I's not a gwine to 'flict 'em, sir, and, sir, I votes no."

The galleries broke out in a cheer. Mr. Azariah Fuller looked chapfallen, but the State was saved.*

* If anybody should fail to find this incident in any reputable Georgia history, they must remember that history doesn't tell everything, but leaves much to our imagination.

CHAPTER XXX.

"GET THEE BEHIND ME, SATAN."

THE convention was over, and the race for a Governor and members of the Legislature was to be had. The leading men of Habersham wanted Roger to run for the House of Representatives. He was not unaspiring. He realized that the times were perilous and the work devolving on the Legislature would be very important, and after he was nominated he was anxious to be elected. His election to the convention had been without opposition, but not so now. He had not reached his position of popular favor without exciting feelings of envy on the part of the less successful.

Young McAtee was a lawyer of a few more years than Roger. He had read Blackstone and a book on Evidence and Cobb's Digest, and had been admitted to the bar. He had read little since that. He knew how to draw a deed, make a will, or sue out a warrant. He was ready for anything, however, which came along, and before the justice of the peace or a petit jury he was really a power. He was, in truth, smart, unscrupulous, and agile. He asked for the nomination of the Democrats to the House, but did not receive it, and announced himself as an independent candidate. He was well known, largely connected, and was hand in hand with the moonshiners. He threw himself into the campaign with all ardor.

Roger was not disposed to neglect opportunities to make himself known and popular. He went to the school exhibitions, he went to the barbecues, he made speeches, he went to the homes of the people; but he positively refused to treat or allow any others to do so for him. His friends became alarmed. McAtee was treating vigorously, and was making headway.

Squire Roberts was one of Roger's constituents, and he became anxious. "See here, Lawson," he said, "this ain't gwine to do. Politics in this country hain't run according to the ten commandments. You've got to lay down a part of your religion till you whip this fight."

"Well, Squire, I can't do it. If the good people of Habersham County want me to represent them, I'll do it; but I am not going to get my seat by a perjury."

"Well, no. But you stand off, and we'll manage for you. You just quit that Sunday school business till after the election, and quit these temperance speakin's, and your friends will fix you."

"No, Squire, no."

"Well, you're the queerest politicianer I ever struck up with. Why, when John Thompson—and he was a locus preacher—was a runnin' for tax collector, he jest went plumb blind and deaf till the election was over."

It was evident Roger was going to be beaten if he continued his course. Col. Billups came to him. "See here, Lawson, you must be elected. Too much depends on it to let scruples stand in the way. I know you are right in principle, but we are now in a war, and all is fair in love and war. There is no moral wrong in simply holding some things in abeyance and allowing some things questionable to be done for greater good."

"But, Colonel, I cannot. I owe you much, but I can't do this; it is wrong."

Roger was to be beaten, so everybody said. The election came on. The vote at Clarksville would settle it. James Bass and the Squire were at work at their precinct and would take care of that. A crowd of Confederate soldiers were on hand in town, and Andy Rhodes, who had come back from the Nation, was there. He had just come in the week before. He had done his best for Roger, and now when the election came on Andy was at work for his friend. The tide seemed against Roger, but there were many friends who stood by him. At last Dr. Phillips said: "Andy, you were born in the cove; you know the boys there; you must make a speech."

"O yes! O yes! O yes! Andy Rhodes is going to make a speech."

The crowd drew near. Andy jumped on a goods box. "Boys," he said, "you know Andy Rhodes is better at fightin' than speakin', and you know he hain't the best man in the world, and he is a leetle too fond maybe of mountain dew; but you know Andy never goes back on a friend. Now Roger Lawson's daddy was rich, and there weren't nobody's daddy poorer than mine; but Capt. Lawson use to speak kind to me when I was a barfoot boy, and when my daddy died he bought the coffin for my old mammy, and when he went to the war I went with him, and out in camp at Cotton Hill I tuck the mumps; and then I had the measles, and come mighty nigh a dyin'; and this here same Roger Lawson, he nussed me like a baby. I was with him when he was shot the fust time, and I tuck him offen the battlefield; and I seed him when he fell at Gettysburg. I know him, and so do you. He's the ginuine stuff.

If Bill McAtee, who is a tryin' to beat him, ever smelt gunpowder, or ever helped a poor man, who ever hearn of it? When the Widder Jenkins was about to lose her land, who saved it for her?"

"Why, Capt. Lawson did, bless his heart!" said an earnest and excited voice, "and I wish I had a hundred votes. He should have every one of 'em." It was the voice of the widow. She had just come to town.

"Boys, will you go back on a one-armed Confed, say will you?"

"No! no! hurrah for Lawson!"

And so Roger went to the Legislature by a handsome majority.

CHAPTER XXXI.

SOME SURPRISES.

IT is not my purpose to tell of Roger's life as a legislator, nor to give a history of that motley body known as the Bullock Legislature. The time has not come, perhaps, to speak of these things dispassionately, and we are not yet, it may be, able to do justice to all concerned; and then, besides, I am not writing a history of events, but telling a story of how one of my young countrymen, by energy and uprightness, overcame the obstacles that were thrown in his way by the unparalleled changes of the war. Nor need I try to conceal the fact that the aim of this little chronicle is to arouse in the hearts of my young countrymen aspirations after noble things, and that my story has a moral. It has been too generally accepted as a truth that young men are to be ruled by passion and appetite; that tenderness to mothers and consideration for sisters and, above all, loyalty to God are not to be expected in the average young man of good position. In these days when young men are divided into two classes—men and society men—I would be glad for my young readers to see, not a faultless young fellow, but one who had genuine piety and a high sense of gentlemanly honor and spirit of honest independence, which he cherished as his next best possession, and who was not to be conquered by difficulties. He was soon found to be a legislator with whom it was useless to lobby, and men who had schemes passed by the young member from Habersham to try their arts elsewhere. The temptations which surrounded the young member of the Legislature were not a few, but it was soon seen that those who kept the private bottle in the committee room, or who formed the Poker Club, which met in the same place, or who went to the disreputable exhibitions, or worse houses, which are always found in a city in which legislative sessions are held, had no attractions for him; nor did the sneers at the Christian statesman, or the Puritan in politics, have any influence over him. But if I keep my promise not to write a history of these, the darkest days Georgia ever saw, I must leave my young legislator in the Opera House in Atlanta, which had just been secured for the use of the government, and go to Habersham to see Helen and her mother. "Ivy Bush" had been wonderfully transformed in these two years. As Roger's means increased he added to the comforts of his mother's home. And old Jack, long his mistress's gardener, too old now to do much more than work around the house, was constantly improving the garden and grounds. Beautiful woodbines had been brought by him from the woods and planted around the front piazza; the sweet shrub and honeysuckle had been transplanted from the woods to the garden; a number of roses, white and red, were in the yard; and the old time flowers, touch-me-nots and jonquils and nasturtiums and hyacinths and tulips and verbenas and pinks and dahlias, were in rich abundance. The neglected orchard had been pruned, and new trees had been planted, and old Jack had made the kitchen garden contribute richly to the comforts of the table. The flocks of geese and ducks which floated so gracefully on the waters of the Sequee, and the crowds of chickens, large and small, and of turkeys, dignified and venerable, told of Helen's thrift and Mammy's care. The triweekly mail brought the *New York Observer* of old times, a little too highly flavored with war seasoning yet, but still the good old *Observer*, and now Roger's *Advocate* and the weekly secular papers came regularly to break anything like seclusion from the world. " Dear Aunt Bass," as Helen called her, was still able to come over and spend the day, and the wife of James came with her and brought her two little girls, who thought Aunt Helen was their kinswoman in reality. The little pony carriage furnished the mother and daughter a conveyance to Salem, where Helen attended the Sunday school, and where James Bass, in Roger's absence, superintended it. She was still a Presbyterian. A Methodist Presbyterian, she pleasantly called herself; but Mr. Wood, the Methodist preacher, was at "Ivy Bush" as often as he was at Squire Bass's, and as much at home there. Was there ever, will there be ever, a sweeter, cleaner, purer society than the country neighborhoods of Georgia used to present, and I hope present us still?

Helen was as happy as a bird. The sick knew her, the poor loved her, and while the rustics stood a little in awe of one who, lady-born, lady-bred, and lady-clad, could not but show what she was, there was not one of the plainest girls who did not respect her, nor one of the boys who would not have died in her defense. The plain, uneducated, badly dressed girls who came from the hills around Salem soon learned that she had no feeling of contempt for them, but was their friend, and her influence told in all the section about. She had one of the outhouses at "Ivy Bush" fitted up, and opened a school, and had a houseful of young pupils.

While she was so faithfully at work there was quite a surprise in store for them all. Gen. Lawson had one hundred shares of Rosevelt Factory stock, counted as worthless, but which he had not disposed of. Judge Hansford, who was President of the company, had time to time written to Roger that he was rebuilding and refurnishing the mill, and had some hope that after all there would be a time, not far in the future, for paying dividends. One day in Atlanta he met Roger. "Well, Captain, I'm glad to say the old Rosevelt is on her feet again. The Directors on Saturday declared a semiannual dividend of three dollars a share, and I will have the Treasurer to send you a check for it to-morrow."

Roger had long wished to return to his old friend, Bingham, the amount of money that he had loaned him, but he had not been able to do so. He resolved to send him this three hundred dollars. He had heard no word from him for three years. Bingham had not written to him, very naturally, for he did not know where he was, and Roger was not willing to write to him in those days of bitter agitation, for he feared lest any approach on his part might have been construed improperly. So he had kept silence; but now he could safely break it, and he wrote to his old friend:

House of Representatives,
Atlanta, Ga., Nov., 1868.

My Dear Yank: I have often thought of you, and how gratefully you can never know, since we parted at Fort Delaware; but you know how a gentleman feels and how impossible it has been for me, during the last three years, to do other than preserve the silence which has marked my course. But while I have said nothing, I assure you that you have had as warm a place in my heart as any living man. But I am not going to afflict you with a long letter, or with sentiment. You were kind enough when I needed it to give me a help which I valued very much then and have been grateful for ever since. I should have made some recognition of your kindness long ago if I could have done so, but nearly all we had was swept away, and I was not able to do as I wished. I am glad to say I can now repay the loan in part, and I inclose you $300, New York exchange.

We are living in a pleasant little home in the mountains, at "Ivy Bush," near Clarksville, in Habersham County. There are only three of us: mother, Helen, and I. Old Jack and Mammy and our old friend, Young Jack, now the happy father of two black cherubs, are with us.

I suppose, of course, you are married; and if you can come South, I wish you would come and see us and bring your wife. You can reach us easily now by a new railroad, the Air Line from Atlanta to Charlotte.

Truly yours. Roger Lawson.

In a week Roger received the following:

Office Binghamton Mills,
Binghamton, Conn., December 7, 1868.

My Dear Johnny: I cannot tell you how glad I was to hear

from you. I have been hoping to get a word from you for all these years. I am almost sorry you remembered the trifling kindness I showed you when you were in want of it. I am glad you are where I knew you would go when I parted from you: at the front.

I am here in the cotton mill. My good father had a large interest in this enterprise, and when he died, which he did two years ago, I was elected President of the company, and am now quite a man of business.

No, I am not married. I wonder where you got that idea. I hope to be some time, when I can find the right kind of a girl, but I have not found her yet. My dear mother and sister Clara are with me, or rather I am with them.

I thank you for the invitation you gave me, and I hope next spring to avail myself of it, as I wish to come South; and then, too, I would like so much to see your mother and sister again. So I think I will take Clara and run down South in May, and stop at "Ivy Bush" to see you.

Give my kindest regards to your mother when you write, and Miss Helen, and don't forget Jack. Congratulate him for me on his propitious marriage.

Truly yours. JOHN H. BINGHAM.

CHAPTER XXXII.

MAY FLOWERS.

WHEN Col. Bingham went home after receiving the letter from Roger he handed it to his sister, who read it to her mother. "Well," said his sister, "are you going?"

"Yes, I am going, and I want you to go with me."

"Me? Why, I am not invited."

"No, but my wife is, and you must take her place."

"Why, my son," said the mother, "you are not in earnest, are you?"

"Yes, mother; I want Clara to see the South, and I have some business with a firm in Atlanta, and must go there, and then I want to see the people who were so kind to me."

"But are you not afraid of the Kuklux? the *Tribune* says that a Northern man's life is in danger in Georgia unless he is a Democrat."

"Yes, so it does, and perhaps it thinks so; but I know that it is not true. So when you go in May to Sister Mary's, I will take Clara with me to

Georgia. When I tell you that Mrs. Lawson is a Presbyterian, and reads the *New York Observer*, you will be willing to trust us in her care, I am sure."

"Yes, I reckon there are some good people down in the unhappy country; and I know that she must be one of them. I can never forget how kind they all were to you, and I think, if you can, you ought to go; but I am afraid that it is a little risky."

The spring months came on, and the proposed journey was made. To the Connecticut maiden the journey was of unceasing interest. She had never been farther south than New York, and now Philadelphia and Baltimore and Washington and Richmond were each visited, and then in the early part of May the cars stopped at Mt. Airy, and the handsome young Federal colonel and his gentle sister stepped off. Roger was there to meet them, and Helen had come with him. She took the stranger girl by the hand, and kissed her as tenderly as if she had been her sister. The meeting of Roger and Bingham was like that of two schoolboys.

The letter from Clara to her mother, however, tells the story better than I can:

"IVY BUSH," HAEERSHAM CO., GA.

My Dear Mother: Well, here I am. I can hardly believe

that I am awake, everything is so strange and new to me. Our journey was an ovation. The hurried letters I sent you can give you but a faint idea of the great pleasure with which a Connecticut girl visits the South for the first time. In Richmond I was delighted beyond measure. I went to the capitol, went into the old library, saw the pictures of the old gentlemen of the colony, visited Libby Prison and Belle Isle, and rode over the battlefields; and after our visit there was over, we took the railroad, going to Danville, and thence through North Carolina and the foothills of the mountains, until we reached Mt. Airy. This is merely a station on the railroad. Clarksville is six miles north of it, and "Ivy Bush," where we are staying, is on the Sequee, three miles from Clarksville.

Helen and her brother were there to meet us. She kissed me like she had known me always, and greeted brother like an old friend. They had an old time carriage, and an old colored man (Uncle Jack, we call him) to drive it. Two fat mules were hitched to it. We did not go very fast, but if our team had been a fast one, the roads would have prevented it, for they are too hilly for fast travel.

We reached "Ivy Bush" about dark. Mrs. Lawson was looking for us. She is a dear old lady, who reminds me very much of you. She has a sweet, sad look on her face, and is very quiet. Poor woman! she has had a world of trouble. Her children are so sweet to her! Capt. Lawson is so thoughtful and gentle, and Helen takes all care from her. Dear old Mammy always calls her child yet, and watches over her like she was a child sure enough.

"Ivy Bush" is the sweetest, sunniest place that you ever saw, and the house as cozy as you would wish. Helen and I have the same room, and so have Capt. Lawson and brother, for the house is not a large one.

They have three servants. Aunt Judy, the cook, has been

with them always, and Mammy used to nurse Mrs. Lawson. Chloe, who does the housework, is the wife of Jack, who took care of brother and Capt. Lawson when they were both wounded. It is just as nice here as it can be, and I am delighted. I will write you more when I see more. I just send you this now.

Affectionately, CLARA.

To a young woman from a New England village, the change to the mountains of Upper Georgia was a striking one, and Clara was thoroughly delighted with all she saw. Indeed, there are few sections of the country which are more attractive, in many of their features, than the mountain country of Upper Georgia; and in the middle of May, when the honeysuckle is in its glory, and robed in white and pink and crimson and orange, it sheds its fragrance to the breeze. When the dogwood is in its bridal robe, when there is the yellow jasmine and the red woodbine, and when the calycanthus with its exquisite perfume, and the red buds, and the grandfather graybeards, and the hawthorn, with the beautiful white clusters, and the fragrant crab apples are everywhere, and when beneath the feet are the violets and trilliums and pink roots and sweetbriers and ladies' slippers and the trailing arbutus, when the mocking bird sings, and the redbird flits like a flash of fire, and bluebirds twitter, and the humming birds dash from flower to flower—when all this was around the fair girl, no wonder she was carried away with delight.

Roger and Bingham, with their fishing rods, for the season of shooting was over, spent their days on the Sequee fishing for the black bass and the salmon trout and the smaller fish which are found in the stream. Bingham could only spend a week or two, and so Roger devoted all his time to him. A part of the time was given up to excursions. They went to the beautiful Nacoochee Valley and to Tallulah. Clara must tell in her letter of these journeys:

"Ivy Bush," May, 1869.

My Darling Mother: I have just returned from a most delightful excursion. Capt. Lawson made up a party to go over to Nacoochee and Mt. Yonah. There were six of us: Capt. Lawson, Mr. Bass, Brother, and Mrs. Bass, Helen, and I. We had fourteen miles to ride, so we began our journey as soon as it was bright enough to see our way. Our road was largely through forests until we reached the Nacoochee Valley, which is about two miles long. The Chattahoochee winds its way like a silver thread through the middle of it. Beautiful forest-covered mountains are on every side of it, and Mt. Yonah, the loftiest of them, where we were going, borders it. We drove up the mountain until we could no longer drive, and then climbed on foot to the top. The view from this point was indescribably grand and beautiful. The vale of Nacoochee, with its charming little farms, nestled like a garden at our feet. The beautiful Chattahoochee wound its way southward. Looking south, as far as the eye could see was an ocean of green; for from the height on which we were it appeared to be an almost unbroken forest. Looking north and east and west, there were mountains, mountains, mountains. The indescribable purplish tint of the nearer ranges faded away into the delicate blue of the far-distant peaks which tower above the blue range in North Carolina and Tennessee. There was no point to which the eye could be turned where there was not grandeur and beauty. We spent the morning on the mountain, and in the afternoon we came back to "Ivy Bush" again. Day after to-morrow we are to go to Tallulah, where Capt. Lawson says I will see the most picturesque scene this side of the Rocky Mountains. I am wonderfully well. My cheeks are tanned a little by being in the sun so much, but my appetite is magnificent, and Aunt Judy tries herself cooking for me.

Lovingly, CLARA.

While Col. Bingham and Roger were watching their corks as they were fishing for salmon trout in the pool below the fall on the river, they talked freely, as they had often done, of the condition of public affairs. Each had found place for a change of view on many subjects, and each with sturdy honesty held to those opinions which he thought were true. That day the question of the tariff and its effects was being discussed. Roger was for free trade; Bingham, for the tariff.

"Johnny," said his friend, "if I were selfish, I would want the tariff protection removed; and if you were selfish, you would certainly wish it retained. Do you know that this part of Georgia is destined to be the great workshop of America?

New England cannot present one-half of the advantages you have here for manufacturing, and our factories are already established, and need no help. Not so here. Take the spot where we are sitting. Here is water power sufficient to run one hundred thousand spindles. It never fails. Here is stone enough at your very door for every building you can wish, and here is timber in the greatest abundance. Here are the people to work the mills at reasonable wages, and here is the cotton right at your door to spin, were your factories already built as ours are. You can make yarn and muslin, and ship it to Binghampton and sell it for twenty-five per cent. profit, and then undersell us if we sold at cost."

"Well, all that, Yank, may be true, but that does not make protection right. But I argue with you as to its benefit to us if we could take advantage of it. But we have no capital; and, as my old friend, Col. Howard, says: 'You can't get a goose to water without capital.'"

"That is true, also, but there is an over abundance of capital in New England. It is timid, but will go where it is safe and where it promises to give a good return. Now, suppose we form a company. You put in this water power and this quarry and fifty acres of land at about $10,000, and I will put up that amount in money, and I am sure I can stock up a company with $100,000 capital."

"Agreed!" said Roger.

"Look out! there goes your cork," and the conversation suddenly came to a halt, as the Connecticut colonel drew a splendid trout to the shore.

The next day the visitors were to go to Tallulah. It was too much of a journey to go and return in a day, so the tourists went the afternoon before and spent the next day at the falls, and of what they saw Clara wrote her mother in an enthusiastic letter. The estimate of the fair maiden will be fully indorsed by any one who ever looked upon Tallulah, which is one of the most unique and magnificent spectacles presented east of the Rocky Mountains. The Tallulah River, which rises in the mountains of Rabun, in Upper Georgia, is a stream of considerable size when, sparkling and bright and free, it dashes into a deep ravine in Habersham. Through this narrow ravine, between mountains of sandstone which tower hundreds of feet above the river bed, the river comes hurrying, at first playfully, then earnestly, then angrily. It meets obstructions in the precipices which cross its channel, then it sweeps on and, foaming in its rage, roaring in its anger, it rushes downward until it loses itself in the grand chasm. No wonder the Indians called it "The Terrible." This great chasm is nearly one thousand feet deep, and on every side tower the walls of the precipice, and in their bosom is embraced the limpid stream, which is now calm and peaceful after its terrific passion. No one can look on such a scene without a thrill and almost an ecstasy of delight.

Clara wrote to her mother:

"Ivy Bush," May.

My Darling Mother: I did not know there was in the world, much less in Georgia, which I have always looked upon as a dreary plain of ponds and pine woods, such a magnificent scene as that which we looked on yesterday. Capt. Lawson told me Tallulah had no equal this side of the Rocky Mountains, and I am sure he is right; and brother says that if he had choice of spending a second week at Niagara or at Tallulah he would take Tallulah every time.

The river is not a large one. It is as clear as crystal and as blue as the sky. It comes sweeping down between high mountains, which slope gradually down about a hundred feet from the river bed, and then become bare precipices. Above this they are covered with cedars and ivy. There are rude pathways made along the stream on one of its banks, and from the brink of the precipice, over which the water dashes, you can look down into the boiling waves, where the rainbow continually flashes in beauty.

At last the river rushes into the grand chasm, an immense amphitheater whose walls are near one thousand feet high. Here we rested, and while Helen and I were gathering pebbles and flowers brother and Capt. Lawson, unpoetic fellows, were trying to catch some fish. I am glad to say they did not succeed.

I cannot begin to describe the scenes around us here. They are in such variety and there is such a mingling of beauty and grandeur that when I begin to write I am bewildered.

We spent several hours in the grand chasm, and had our lunch there, and then we began the task of climbing out. There is only one way of egress, where the rocks are not bare and steep. It requires a climb of nearly a mile to get back to the heights again. We were thoroughly done up when we reached the road. We had a pleasant ride homeward, and reached "Ivy Bush" about dark.

I can't tell you what a pleasant time I have had with these kind-hearted Southerners. Brother and Capt. Lawson sit down and talk about the war and shooting at each other, just as if it was nothing; and when Col. Billups came out to spend an evening he was just as kind to brother as if they had been in the same army.

Let me tell you of something which touched me very much. The other day Helen had gone to see a sick neighbor, and brother and Capt. Lawson had gone to the village to fix up some papers, and I was sitting under the oak tree in an easy-chair reading, when the gate opened and I saw a regular Georgia "cracker." She was dressed in a dress of yellow homespun made in the style of a hundred years ago. She had on a sun-bonnet of cheap calico; her shoes were brogans. She had a hard face, but a kindly one, and had a very bright eye. She evidently took me for Helen. She came up to me and said in a very curious tone: "Is you Capt. Lawson's sister?"

"No, ma'am; I'm a stranger."

"You is? Whar is you from?"

"From Connecticut."

"Connecticut? whar is that?"

"Why away up North."

"What? is you a yankee?"

"Well, that's what they call us."

"Well, the yankees killed my husband, and he never done 'em no harm. Is you Capt. Lawson's folks?"

"No, only his friend."

"Well, ef you is his friend, I is your friend."

"You like him, then?"

"Like him! I love the very ground he walks on, and you would not wonder as I do ef you knowed what he's dun for me."

"What did he do?" I said.

"Well, when I was a pore widder with four little childern and my daddy was dead and old Bill Hillborn stole my land, Capt. Lawson got it back for me, and I never paid him a cent, and old Bill Hillborn could have almost made him rich. I hain't been able to do nothin' for him yit, but I knit these socks this winter and I've brung 'em to him. As his sister hain't here, I wish you would give 'em to him."

She handed me a half-dozen pairs of plain, country-knit socks as her present. It was a rather awkward thing for a young lady to give such a present to a gentleman, and when Helen came I handed the quaint gift to her with the message of love the woman had left for him.

You need not smile. I certainly am not in love with the unreconstructed young rebel; but it is not often you see one more worthy of a woman's love. Helen is a jewel, but how they could be other than what they are with such a mother I could hardly see.

Our visit is nearly at an end. To-morrow we are going to Atlanta, and thence to Savannah and by steamer to New York. Brother sends love.

Affectionately,

CLARA.

The last night of the stay of the visitors had come. They were on the porch of the cottage sitting under the woodbines. The honeysuckle vine breathed its fragrance on the air, and the gentle breeze from the hills brought the sweet odor of the wild grape on its bosom. The moon was full, and the moonbeams came softly through the vines. The young people had just come from the sitting room, where Roger had held the evening family worship, and now they sat there on the vine-covered porch. There were the rustic seats in the front yard under two large oaks, and they went out into the yard and occupied them. What they said to each other as they sat there in the moonlight I never knew. Indeed, I think that eavesdropping is not the proper thing to do. I simply know that they talked long and softly. The weird notes of the whip-poor-will came from the grove, and the low murmur of the waterfall fell on the ear. The sky was bright, the air was balmy, the young people were susceptible, and if anything had happened it would not have been a strange event.

Col. Bingham looked somewhat thoughtful that night, and said little. And the next day when they parted at Mt. Airy there was a strange reserve in Helen's manner toward him, while her warm embrace told Clara of her sadness at her going.

"Johnny, old fellow," Bingham said, "you do not know how much I have enjoyed this reunion. May the union of our hearts be typical of the union of this sadly divided country! Come to Connecticut, and let me show you that a cold-blooded yankee has a warm place in his heart for even an unmitigated rebel such as you are."

The cars moved off, and there was a real feeling of loss at "Ivy Bush" when the visitors were gone.

CHAPTER XXXIII.

ORANGE FLOWERS.

THE mail to Clarksville came now every day, and almost every other day Miss Helen Lawson received a letter from somebody, I don't know who. I never read these letters, nor did I read those written in a lady's hand which went to Col. J. H. Bingham, at Binghamton, Conn.

I heard some very ill-natured things said about the way Col. Bingham had been treated at "Ivy Bush," but they were said by Bill McAtee. He said that "any man who would treat the enemy of his country as Roger Lawson had treated Col. Bingham, instead of being in the Legislature ought to be in the penitentiary."

Andy Rhodes heard him say it, and in his quaint way he said, with some expressions I omit: "Bill McAtee, you've never got over Roger Lawson's a beatin' you for the Legislature. Now, you'd better dry up! Everybody knows that you hid out o' the war, and got among Joe Brown's pets, and never done nothin' but grumble; and I jist tell you that Roger Lawson is too much of a gentleman to notice you; but Andy Rhodes hain't, and if you want to keep his hands offen you, you jest keep your tongue offen Roger Lawson!"

Roger had gone on steadily in his work. Col. Billups took him into partnership, and the firm of Billups & Lawson was the leading firm of lawyers in the upcountry.

I was on my circuit when I received this letter from Roger. It was written in October, 1869:

My Dear Parson: My Sister Helen expects to be married to Col. J. H. Bingham, of Connecticut, on the 30th inst. She desires, as we all do, that you should perform the ceremony. Come over to "Ivy Bush," and go with us to the church at Salem, where she is to be married.

Affectionately your old friend,   Roger Lawson.

I reached Mt. Airy, where I was to meet Roger, and found Col. Bingham and his sister. They were going to Clarksville, and expected to come out the next day to "Ivy Bush." The express agent called to Roger, and said: "I have some packages for you." And there were a number evidently containing wedding presents. Several small packages were marked "valuable," and were directed to Miss Helen Lawson. One of them came from Binghamton, Conn.

When they reached home Roger handed his sister the package from Connecticut, and when she opened it there were the *jewels that her father had given her*. In addition to them, there was a beautiful watch. This was a present from the groom.

The secret was now out. The yankee officer who was in Savannah was Col. Bingham, and the jewels had been bought for the bride when the time should come that she should be his.

There was a box for Mrs. Lawson. One may know at once what it had in it. The Lawson silver was at home again. It had on it a simple card: "With the grateful love of John H. Bingham."

The next day a little congregation met at Salem, the country church. The wife of James Bass and the school children had decorated the little church with evergreens, and a congregation of loving neighbors had come to the wedding. Roger and Clara stood beside the sister, and Aunt Bass and Uncle Bass sat each near the loving mother, and I, the old chaplain of Col. Lawson's regiment, read the beautiful service of our Church and married the young folks, and never did I do that with a firmer assurance than that this " holy estate had been entered into reverently, discreetly, and in the fear of God."

Aunt Judy was at home fixing up for the wedding dinner, but Mammy and Uncle Jack were here at the church, and among those who gave their hands in congratulation there were none more hearty than dear old Mammy and dear Uncle Jack.

A small party—Squire Bass and his wife, and James Bass and his wife, and Col. Billups and his family—gathered around the table at "Ivy Bush" to a sumptuous dinner which Aunt Judy and Chloe had prepared, and Jack in all his glory was present to welcome the guests and wait on the table.

Among the many gifts was a gorgeous brooch from "Hon. Robert Lawson, Esq., of Liberty County, to Miss Helen Lawson, with his compliments." Bob's taste was not the best, but his motives were the kindest.

The bride and groom and Clara went on a long bridal tour to Florida, Mobile, and New Orleans; and then to Connecticut, where the good old mother and sister of Col. Bingham welcomed the Southern bride with genuine tenderness.

The factory company was formed and the "Ivy Bush Factory" was established, and after a few years Col. Bingham left Connecticut and came to Georgia and manages the mill.

Roger did not marry Clara as you expected (she married the Congregational minister in Binghamton), but Miss Mary Billups. He was long ago elected the judge of his circuit, and is trusted and loved and honored by all his people. He is to-day a Confederate veteran, but while on the best terms with those who wore the blue, is never ashamed to tell of the deeds of the " boy in gray; " and nothing delights Helen's two "yankee boys," as she calls them, more than to hear Uncle Roger tell of his adventures, unless it is for the two rebel sons of Roger to hear their Uncle John tell of the deeds of the " boy in blue."

And now, under the somewhat flimsy covering of a fiction, I have tried to tell the boys and girls not exactly what I saw and felt, but what did occur during the war and after it. If one should ask is who the real hero of this story, I perhaps could not tell him. The fathers of my readers can possibly call up the memory of more than one who bore at least some part such as Roger bore, and possibly their mothers knew of more than one Helen who bravely bore her part as well.

I trust our children will all remember that at fearful cost we their fathers settled some questions that they must never allow to be opened, and the one settled forever is the fearful danger of sectionalism. The strife which began in 1832 in a bitter war of words between the South and the North reached its natural end in the clashing of swords thirty years after that. This is our country—North, South, East, West—all ours, and the blood and treasure it has cost has been poorly spent if our children do not see it so.

www.ingramcontent.com/pod-product-compliance
Lightning Source LLC
Chambersburg PA
CBHW032138230426
43672CB00011B/2382